FOLK
PHENOMENOLOGY

FOLK PHENOMENOLOGY

Education, Study, and the Human Person

SAMUEL D. ROCHA

PICKWICK *Publications* · Eugene, Oregon

FOLK PHENOMENOLOGY
Education, Study, and the Human Person

Pickwick Publications
An Imprint of Wipf and Stock Publishers
199 W. 8th Ave., Suite 3
Eugene, OR 97401
www.wipfandstock.com

ISBN 13: 978-1-4982-2084-2

Cataloging-in-Publication data:

Rocha, Samuel D.

Folk phenomenology : education, study, and the human person.

xvi + 134 p. ; cm. Includes bibliographical references.

ISBN 13: 978-1-4982-2084-2

1. Eduction 2. Phenomenology. I. Title.

ED2635.8 R26 2015

Manufactured in the U.S.A.

To my beautiful children: Tomas, Gabriel, and Sofia.

"From what rests on the surface one is led into the depths."
EDMUND HUSSERL

"I beg you to escape, and live, and hear all of the real."
GIL SCOTT-HERON

Contents

Foreword

by William F. Pinar

SAM ROCHA SAYS THIS book is for teachers not dreamers, but I'm not so sure. After all, he defines phenomenology[1] as "nothing more than imagining the real."[2] The real is simultaneously close-at-hand and distant, what is visible and what is not, what we can hear and what we suspect is sounding if we could only attune ourselves to its frequency.[3] "Even the body"—which Rocha takes as "a phenomenological first instance from existence"—"operates in its own times, spaces, and manners." Like the real itself, the body seems to have a mind of its own.

"I am an erotic person," Rocha confides, "because eros is first and foremost ontological, and therefore must be more potent, fecund, and real than symbols, words, grammar, and the epistemological accounts they prescribe. Even if meaning melts away, eros will remain, silently, in the dark."[4] Here eros is not conflated with the extra-discursive but certainly

---

1. Not only in the philosophy of education (see, for instance, Denton, *Existentialism and Phemomenology in Education*) has phenomenology enjoyed a long history. In 1977, theorizing a political economy of curriculum, Huebner (in *Lure of the Transcendent*, ed. Vikki Hillis) suggested that "a phenomenological methodology would help, in which the investigator brackets out his/her own taken-for-granted realties and indeed turns to consciousness of the 'thing itself.'" His advice was very much taken up by scholars in curriculum studies, especially in Canada (see, for instance, Aoki, "Sonare and Videre").

2. Unless otherwise indicated, all quoted passages are from *Folk Phenomenology*.

3. Rocha is also a musician, a guitarist and singer. "What singing means," Friedrich Kittler asserts, is "binding, enchanting with love, knowing." Kittler reminds us that the "word 'music' derives from *muse*, even in Arabic" (See Kittler, *Truth of the Technological World*, 260).

4 Friedrich Kittler writes: "The essence of the human being involves, before all knowledge, moods" (see Kittler, *Truth of the Technological World*). Rocha knows: "We cannot

inhabits it, less an identifiable domain than what exceeds our capacities for comprehension.[5]

"In and through these studies," Rocha alerts us, "I am led to believe that that there is reason to be hopeful for something new out there, that there is ever-ancient and ever-new beauty to find, become, and be-with and within." Like "hope," education becomes the "insatiable desire for something real and true." Coming upon that "something" doesn't end desire, however, as "Being's only invitation seems to be into infinity." Yet, it is not otherworldly, at least not only: "Being is never ahistorical, it is the very condition upon which history becomes possible. This worldly notion of Being does not make it any less mysterious." What it does make of it is more desirable: "Education as mystery reveals education as more, not less, desirable." Study is an erotic pursuit in this sense.[6] "The power of a real and true absence is remarkably erotic and tragically powerful," Rocha affirms.

There is, Rocha writes, a "particular affinity between phenomenology and ontology." Not only can phenomenology enable us to focus on "the things themselves"—like "joy"—but "even the phenomenon of Being itself." Indeed, Rocha asserts, "phenomenological knowledge is itself ontological."[7] No straightforward expression of intentionality,[8] Rocha's phenomenology means "moving inward through a gentle caress (like evaporation) of the imagination to intensify them [the things themselves] and render them more radically saturated as they are." Not "going out of tune,"[9] such re-

---

separate our communal and social life from our innermost thoughts, feelings, and desires."

5. "Eros does not submit itself to interpretation," Rocha writes. "It is a question of being as opposed to meaning."

6. "Study, then, is like other forms of eros: a wild thing, partly this and partly that, teeming with fortune." Rocha terms his view an "erotic theory of study."

7. Working within Chinese cultural traditions, Chen Xiangming and her colleagues characterized the teaching they observed as "ontological," and the teachers with whom they worked regarded their teaching "as something requiring a synergy of heavenly blessing, worldly advantage and human harmony," no simplistic adaptation of technique nor teaching to the test (see Chen Xiangming, "Meaning-Making of Chinese Teachers"; quoted passages in Zhang and Pinar, *Autobiography and Teacher Development*).

8. Rocha sees himself making "a corrective suggestion to phenomenological approaches that rely on intentionality as the primary or sole force of reduction and replace it (intentionality) with the complexities of subsistence. In place of purely intentional accounts of study, I will describe study that subsists erotically, that lives in and through desire, but also within a subsistent ecology of fortune." Describing phenomenology, Maxine Greene depicts "consciousness" itself as "characterized by intentionality" (see Maxine Greene, *Teacher as Stranger*, 131).

9. "Once the visionary capabilities associated with the eye, sight, and light—and, by

duction renders what it caresses "more robust and focused expression of itself. Ontological fidelity." Fidelity to being-in-the-world, eschewing "that ancient and dangerous fruit: metaphysics and pure essentialism." Phenomenology, Rocha knows, "is impossible without a genealogy that makes it necessary and prescient for the times we live in."[10]

Rocha outlines the "alarmist" history of public debate over U.S. schooling, noting "the unmistakably apocalyptic tone to these warnings sold as reform." In our time "Education has become messianic."[11] "Schoolvation" is the promise of heaven on earth, provided one's test scores suffice.[12] He is being critical here of messianism but not education, which he locates less institutionally than ontologically.[13] Those scores and the quantification of, well, everything, may be compensatory, for "this much is clear," Rocha writes, "*education remains a mystery to us.*"[14] That mystery has to do with "frustrated desire." For what? "What it is we long for," Rocha reminds us, is "the hope to become a person."

What's *that*? Rocha provides Greek and Roman definitions, now merged (or is it convoluted?) in what he terms the "most radical human invention of all time: the autonomous individual, now fading into the *homo*

---

extension, with their Enlightenment heritage—have exhausted themselves as potentially liberatory instruments," Gerhard Richter writes, "the auditory possibilities of the ear still hold out promise" (see Richter, *Thought-Images*). Ted Aoki concurs (see Aoki, "Sonare and Videre").

10. Invoking genealogy—often associated with Foucault—and the historical moment makes Rocha's embrace of phenomenology almost seem a pragmatism. For a link between Foucault's conception of genealogy and Dewey's pragmatism, see Koopman, *Genealogy as Critique*.

11. This is a point affirmed and extended to democracy by Tzvetan Todorov, who points out that "messianism, this policy carried out on behalf of the good and the just, does both a disservice." He adds: "Democracy has grown sick with its own excesses, freedom is turning into tyranny, the people are becoming an easy-to-manipulate mass, the desire to promote progress is turning into a crusade." These are the "inner enemies" of democracy which it itself has created (see Torodov, *Inner Enemies of Democracy*, 180–81). Among these is school reform (see Pinar, *What Is Curriculum Theory?*, 223).

12. The fervent intensity of school reform signals, it seems, that the school is "dead." But, Rocha writes, "the death of school presents a useful litmus test for studying the metaphysics of education."

13. "Is our notion of 'education' wild and fertile enough," he asks, "to endure and exceed the endangered and domesticated era we live in?"

14 For Alan Block, too, "study is an engagement with the mysteries of the world" (see Block, *Talmud, Curriculum, and the Practical*, 219).

economicus."[15] It is this "invention," he declares, that "inaugurates what Foucault regards to be 'the death of Man.'" Rocha's point is less historical than ontological: *individuals do not exist.* Relationality is in fact "irreducible."[16] Not only do "we arrive, at birth, in relationship, covered in blood," but subjective singularity is always already a multiplicity: "The human person is a public unto herself, from womb to tomb." To put the matter another way, the person is an "existential plurality" within "the erotic proximity of existence."

What the teacher can offer, then, is not "a public institutional identity." Rather, what the teacher offers is "her own human personhood," a mode of being "that also begins as a public." But the "public" the teacher personifies is not so much the site of spirited debate—although subjectivity can be that too—as it is a lived space of "existential intimacy" in which to "offer true love is to be a tragic lover." The teacher—as human person—is "thrown into the flux of relations in the world of Being, the subsistent life-world, embodied in an amorous and tragic way, come what may."

Within this "wider context of Being,"[17] teaching becomes revelation. If "mystery causes us to desire disclosure," is it surprising that teaching is the "art of showing," an exhibitionistic phrasing, I thought at first. But "showing" isn't exclusively visual. It can mean: (1) display, (2) type of performance, or (3) a presentation of facts. The last is a commonplace of teaching, the second is in sync with theories of performativity often associated with the celebrated work of Judith Butler, and the first—display—can connote the visual, but it can also suggest intellectual and psychological disclosure. Rocha seems to have something sacred in mind: "showing is made possible by the offering." Offerings are gifts[18] of course; they can also be rites of contrition and celebration, gifts for gods.[19]

---

15. "Neoliberalism," Tzvetan Todorov points out, "shares with Marxism the belief that the social existence of men depends mainly on the economy" (see Torodov, *Inner Enemies of Democracy*, 90).

16. Nancy Luxon concurs: "Solitary individuals are not to be taken as a starting point; the relations that bind them to one another are." I would point out that relations are among individuals. Here my difference with Rocha is terminological: my "individual" is his "human person" (see Luxon, *Crisis of Authority*, 179).

17. Being is not only "wider," but "dark and wild." Such "unknown forces and energies that drive us to study in our (un)conscious life," Rocha explains.

18. Rocha is wary of the gift. "The struggle [is] to show what has been offered," he writes, "with the hope that never creates the expectation of a gift."

19. "The erotics of study," Rocha explains, "mediate between the human person and the world through the particular ontological passion that calls from beyond and within."

"The teacher never knows for certain that the offering is given," Rocha writes. In fact, "the exchange is never clear or even real." Here is acknowledgement that concepts of "outcomes" can't be quantified, as they are layered and often deferred.[20] Nor does the teacher have a right to expect to know how the offering is received, as Rocha admits only "the hope of showing something real, a hope without expectation or confirmation." That hope seems to reside in—to emanate from—the presence of the teacher, an offering that can be beautiful. "When the offering is shown," Rocha writes, "beauty emerges." He is here more hopeful[21] than I, or, perhaps more precisely, he is more philosophical, as when he insists that "when a lesson or a homily or a routine or a scale is complete, these are the only questions: What was offered? What was shown?" For me these questions not only usher in empiricism, but history, culture, politics, ethics, and metaphysics as well, themselves at times overlapping.[22] As expressions of "folk phenomenology," his questions contain these categories; they provoke like a prism, disclosing a different hue at each angle.

Folk phenomenology, we learn, is "a way to imagine the real, gleaned from pages and experiences and ideas, but most of all from persons, wrestled together through the art of writing and editing." Rocha offers folk phenomenology to the "teacher who feels the anxiety of these times and also the joy, in the only way the offering is ever made: in love, in love, in love, with all the tragedy and life that love brings." Love is the consummation of this offering: "In the end, it disappears as knowledge and becomes something like understanding, something you can understand without knowing. Love."[23] Rocha's folk phenomenology provides passage from knowledge to understanding to love.[24]

20. Not only outcomes, but Being itself is layered: "One of the perplexing curiosities of Being is that it often resembles a never-ending Russian doll or an eternal onion."

21. As the title of chapter 5 confirms, Rocha is not so hopeful as to be naive.

22. "Phenomenology is not timeless," Rocha knows. "Phenomenology is not immune from history or politics."

23. For Rocha, "understanding" is "the desire to know and be known ontologically." For me, that knowledge occurs through study, the ongoing engagement of alterity. Such engagement is informed by the extra-discursive, what Rocha terms the world's mystery, but it is threaded through human thought and emotion, including their formalization and reconstruction in the academic disciplines.

24. See Ephesians 3:19. The theological ground of Rocha's philosophy of education is also explicit in his assertion of a "trinitarian lens of Being, subsistence, and existence." Such a lens, he writes, is "a way of seeking, sensing, and seeing things as they are." A religious order of the Roman Catholic Church, the Trinitarians are a religious family

For Rocha, such movement is a matter of being-in-the-world, "most vividly and consistently revealed in our passions and erotic life." Not sexual[25] necessarily, "desire" demands presence, seeking, study.[26] "Desire is fundamental," he emphasizes, but the eros[27] it references "begins with the simple fact that we desire to be something: *something instead of nothing.*" That "something" is not identity, or anything static for that matter; it is

> the enormous task of being and dwelling within Being, living, and existing by seeking, sensing, and seeing with a fierce and radical fidelity to the absolute reality of our most profound desire: our desire for love and *theosis*, the desire for Desire.

Eros is what enables Tomas to refuse his father's teasing of him.[28] Not psychoanalytic[29] resistance, Rocha insists, but ontological, the substratum of human experience, as even "the most banal and mundane desires hide a deeper and more potent reality that gives way to the dark, pregnant womb of eros." Is the teacher—like the parent[30]—a midwife to the human person seeking to be born?

What is elusive in English becomes clarified in Spanish. In Spanish, Rocha writes, there is a difference between the two expressions for "I am": *soy* ("I am") and *estoy* ("I am"). *Soy* "speaks in an existential voice," he explains, "while *estoy* can only speak from experience and often speaks in

dedicated to a ministry of charity and redemption, committed "to help all who suffer uncommon hardships, especially those who suffer for their faith or who are poor" (see http://www.trinitarians.org).

25. Even "Freud's own conception of eros," Luxon notes, was "as creation rather than eroticism" (see Luxon, *Crisis of Authority*).

26. For Rocha "study must be associated with being within Being, subsisting, and existing," and it "subsists as an erotic force that comes and goes, but never leaves us altogether." Indeed, "without eros," Rocha writes, "there is no learning." Discussing the Talmud, Alan Block asserts that "the goal of this eros is to make a holy people" (see Block, *Talmud*).

27. Quoting Lynne Huffer, Luxon writes that eros is "the name we can give to an ethical practice of embodied subjectivity in relation to truth . . . eros is both ancient and always changing" (see Luxon, *Crisis of Authority*).

28. Rocha writes: "He [Tomas] is asking me to do the impossible: to love him totally as he is, subsists, and exists, all at once."

29. Rocha writes: "It [the challenge presented to him by his son] is not important simply because he is my son and I am his father."

30. "Only when I can begin to seek, sense, and see him [his son Tomas] in this way," Rocha writes, "will I be able to love him—to understand who he is and be present to him." In what way? "Closely."

term of 'I have.'" "*Tengo hambre*" ("I have hunger") is a way to say "*Estoy hambriento*" ("I am hungry"). "*Soy hambriento*" is nonsensical, except if desire is lack—as it is for Lacan—and then that ontological substratum is indeed hunger.

Spanish also clarifies the crucial concept of knowledge. Rocha explains that *saber* is a form of the verb "to know" that references "information or data: knowing *about* things." In contrast, *conocer* means "the knowledge of things themselves." I draw a somewhat similar distinction between "information" (anonymous, just the facts please) and "knowledge" (bearing the imprint of author, place, and time). The two terms blur but in Spanish the distinction is clear: "*Saber* is to know-about. *Conocer* is to know." For Rocha, the former references "epistemological knowledge," while the latter "at least approaches ontological knowledge." For him, it is ontological knowledge that yields understanding.

Perhaps this distinction—between *saber* and *conocer*—informs Rocha's emphasis upon the human person and, specifically, his posing of the teacher's key question: "'Who?'—*Who shall we teach?*"[31] I share Rocha's sense that "human persons are something of an endangered species." That danger derives, in part, from the refusal to know the ontological. The catastrophes behind and before us—in front of us now—may ensure that the lover qua teacher is condemned to be "tragic," but, as Rocha also suggests, the teacher is inspired, "possessed by the erotics of study" and "the irreducible posture" of the parent. Rocha says teacher, but I think the posture of the parent may convey even more clearly what is "irreducible" in the posture of the teacher, namely the resolve to recognize that Tomas is not a goose.

Surely Rocha is right when he asserts that the "existential question of teaching is also the question of 'who." He adds: "The other questions we might ask—what, where, or how—are ordered by this question."[32] But as maybe he would also agree, the "who" informing our reply to the curriculum question are not only those actually existing children we find in our classrooms; they are also those who have preceded us, and those who will follow. Is it not within History that ontology reveals itself to us as human?[33]

31. While recognition is crucial, for me it cannot occur apart from academic knowledge. Perhaps because I position teaching as supplemental to study, I assert the canonical curriculum question—what knowledge is of most worth?—as the teacher's (and student's) central question.

32. For me these questions blur, one into the other, but I subsume them within the curriculum question. On that point Rocha and I disagree.

33. Perhaps History affirms the "folk" in Rocha's phenomenology. "The cacophony of

"We must struggle for love against nihilism," Rocha appeals, but he seems to sense that the struggle is Sisyphean. Education, Rocha concludes, is "the site of hope for tragic transformation for those who dwell in it and suffer its fortune and existential reality." In the pages that follow, Rocha shows us the site.

---

voices," Luxon writes, "helps us to recognize that our personal, ethical vocabularies are woven together from many different languages, different periods of time, different logics and commitments" (see Luxon, *Crisis of Authority*).

One

The Folkloric Reversal

This human drama without a villain or a pang; this community so refined that ice-cream soda-water is the utmost offering it can make to the brute animal in man; this city simmering in the tepid lakeside sun; this atrocious harmlessness of all things, I cannot abide with them.

WILLIAM JAMES, "WHAT MAKES LIFE SIGNIFICANT?"

THE SEARCH

THE POPUL VUH, A Mayan creation myth, traces the origins of the human person to primordial corn. The ancient Greeks, along with innumerable other peoples and wisdom traditions, relied on governing ideas rooted in elements like water, fire, and air. On Ash Wednesdays, Roman Catholics receive a cruciform dab of ashes—burnt palm leaves—on their foreheads, an elemental sign that traces them back to the dirt of Genesis creation stories, that reminds them of the physiological relationship between the human person and the earth, visible after death. Our bodies decompose. We physically become dirt. This is surely the first and last reduction. Death is the ultimate hegemon.

While the elemental and ecological relationship between people and the planet they inhabit is evident in physiological ways, it seems less apparent today in terms of our collective and even cosmic origins. The big bang is compelling not only for its scientific merits, but also because it is a genesis

1

story with ontogenetic claims to make about the world. It places us into the universe within the time of "the beginning."

Searching for origins, from the morbid to the cosmic, from natural death to deep time, is hardly metaphysical in an exclusively philosophical sense. Originating acts—acts of creation—are never entirely new or created from without. A *creatio ex nihilo* requires a *deus ex machina*. There is something strangely familiar about these mysteries, and the ideas, thoughts, and new forms of creation they create in us.

This search for origins, from "the end" of the grave to "the beginning" of time, is certainly not a simple matter of logic. The idea that the logical or mathematical foundations of language (or matter) capture even a shadow of what we are really looking for in this perennial quest is to, at the very least, mistake the external for the internal. It is a search for a padlock combination instead of what is hidden inside the chest, or, perhaps, it is simply to mistake one thing for another. Of course, the reduction of things to these sorts of conceptual atomic properties is in many respects similar to the elemental ones mentioned earlier, but not in this key respect: the concrete cannot be wholly idealized. Flesh remains flesh. This is why theories of purely logical and mathematical composition, not to mention their scientific derivatives, seem to constantly run against the more ordinary experience of the world through the senses and the imagination. This is also why theories of extreme materiality and singularity, such as the so-called New Materialism and Object-Oriented Ontology, always seem prone to the same mistake from the other direction. The zero-sum duel between the real and the ideal is a tail-chasing folly, like "subject versus object" debates and so many other philosophical chestnut contests. Perhaps the only thing more mistaken than these approaches, and their corresponding dialectics, is when the ideas themselves become idealized, twice removed and detached: politics that are politicized and policed into ideologies, with prescriptions, norms, rules, laws, and popular pieties to follow. In the grips of contrived orthodoxy, everything is made cheap and easy.

In the extreme, all fails. The problem with ancient mythopoesis, with religious myths, stories, poems, and songs, is this: they are untrue when taken literally and unimaginatively, and constantly risk floating into nonsense, nuttery, and fundamentalism. The problem with modern scientific claims, even mathematical and logical ones, is this: they are reductionistic when swallowed whole, often taking things literally and unimaginatively, and always risk placing burdens and weight upon things that are foreign to them in the very first and last place. But, to avoid self-defeating imbalance, each of these unique risks also conceal real rewards. The problem with ideology, by contrast, is total: it is parasitic, derivative of both (myth and science), living in the absence of either, with fidelity to neither. We are in a devastating predicament, caught between sentimentalists, rigorists, and nihilists: fundamentalists and New Agers, positivists and psychological dogmatists, postmodernists and poststructuralists. There is either too little to hold on to, too much, or nothing at all. Proportion, attunement, and balance have been neglected. And still, untouched by shallow tides of convention and theoretical trends and moralisms, the desires for, and stories and ideas of, our inevitable mortal end and the beginning of everything multiply, recycle, and endure. And abound. Hope is alive, everywhere.

HISTORY

This situation can be seen in perhaps a different way, through a historical gloss. In the Middle Ages, philosophy was the servant of *theology*, the queen of the sciences at that time. At the outset of modernity, the sovereignty of God was replaced by natural reason so, naturally, philosophy in a very real sense became servant to the *natural sciences*. Today, in late modernity, the neoliberal authority of global capital and consumer markets has replaced the sovereignty of reason, so it seems fitting that philosophy has become servant to the *social sciences*, most of all economics and psychology.[1] Nowhere could this be more real than in the academic field called Education, where social science threatens to become an uncontested form of common sense. Of course it is also true that philosophy has fiercely opposed these eras and their respective *raison d'être*, but the general point remains: philosophy is not immune to power or temporality, and rarely, if ever, has it existed in the position from which it could make a claim to autarky.[2]

When Edmund Husserl inaugurated phenomenology (inspired by the work of his teacher, Franz Brentano) at the turn of the 20th century there was a philosophical mood in Europe and the Americas that found

1. This gloss is interesting for another reason: the eras of theology, science, and now social science were preceded by earlier eras (i.e., the Patristic period for theology, the early modern period for science, the 19th century for social science) when philosophy and theology/science/social science were indistinguishable and inseparable from each other.

2. The question of education—what it might be, what it might be for, and so on—has not been unaffected by this history, either, but, as we will see, that is a far more difficult matter to understand in a serious and sensible way.

the metaphysics of the Ancients, Scholastics, and Early Modernity severely lacking. The mood was widespread across philosophical thinkers, traditions, and schools of thought.[3] Collectively, philosophy seemed poised for the next century, an entry into late modernity and possibly postmodernity, an experiment in a new kind of radical thought, rooted in concrete realities (e.g., logic, math, lived experience, one's sense of existing, ordinary language, physical and psychological behavior and function, and so on). Whatever one might think about the various strands of positivism that exist nowadays, there was something "positivistic," in the sense of being opposed to abstractions at the outset of inquiry, about this time and its now recently passed future. The question that remains today, standing in the early shadow of the past century, is not whether this anti-metaphysical departure was "effective" or even worthwhile in a more general way, but, instead, whether it was a metaphysical departure at all. We might even wonder whether it was a radical, albeit ironic, return to what preceded metaphysics.

In many ways this question—the question of what to do with metaphysics after its demise, and whether that is even possible—was the key motivation for the development of the systematic forms of phenomenology. Husserl's first transcendental reduction sought to return to "things themselves" and render a more exact and complete account and analysis of *objects*; Martin Heidegger's critique of Husserl transitioned from the first reduction of the object into the second reduction of *being* (i.e., the ways of being that things themselves are, fundamentally intertwined in the subjective experience of human existence and the meaning of Being); in Jean-Luc Marion's third reduction we see Being reduced to *givenness* (i.e., the donation through which Being shows itself and is given). These reductions share a similar intuitive circuitry, spirit, and purpose that never depart entirely from Husserl's initial salvo, "To the things themselves!" Yet, in each individual case, including other phenomenological systems (e.g., Max Scheler's ethical personalism, Emmanuel Levinas's ethics of the "Other," Maurice Merleau-Ponty's sensorial accounts of perception, and many more), the scope of phenomenology is ultimately *philosophical*.

Nonetheless, many outside of academic philosophy have found the tradition of phenomenology useful, from the humanities to the social sciences and even in applied and professional fields of psychotherapy and

---

3. In this book I will rely chiefly upon what I hope to show more fully in future work: an appreciation and understanding of the life and work of William James within the spirit and mood of this period, marking a still unplowed terrain of thought in the continental Americas.

medicine. I write from a peculiar position, too, as a "philosopher of education." While these extensions and applications may seem like an unqualified good for phenomenological research, it also risks all the dangers of translation. Most notably, perhaps, in qualitative social science research there is often a severe lack of understanding of phenomenology, most apparent when it is instrumentalized, treated as a "theoretical framework" or, worst of all, a predetermined "method." In my own field, much like in philosophy proper, phenomenology often becomes tantamount to intellectual history, and this repeats the prevalent category mistake that confuses philosophers with philosophy. So, again, we seem to find ourselves in the same hard/ soft predicament, between philosophical rigorism and interdisciplinary instrumentalism.

ART PRECEDES METAPHYSICS

This book seeks to intervene into this situation, described in the previous two sections, by attempting to make a single claim: *art precedes metaphysics*. To assert "art precedes metaphysics" implies that art exceeds metaphysics in the sense that it comes first in the order of things. The reasoning for this is literal and unsophisticated, verging on anthropological: it seems rather obvious that the work of art, the craft of making things, is much older, in both chronological and phenomenological time, than the work of philosophy, which began with "first philosophy," another term for metaphysics.

Another way to show this claim is through what may be the simplest and most immediate ontological comparison: we constantly find ourselves *being* things that we do not *know*. In fact, to be a human person is, in a very real sense, to not know what or who one is. These are the sorts of things that can only be agreed upon initially if a person is already inclined to agree with them, but they reveal part of what is real about the claim "art precedes metaphysics." Even before metaphysics begins, and long after it ends, there is the naked presence of what is around, what is there. We might call this "the real" or any other name we like, but the *presence* of it is not hard to see and hear and touch and feel. And, even if my claim about art and metaphysics remains suspicious (as it obviously should), there is another reason for taking it seriously: the folkloric reversal.

To make the claim "art precedes metaphysics" in a *philosophical* way requires a number of steps that would include articulating a governing theory of art, also known as aesthetics. This is precisely the sort of step that

5

the folkloric reversal seeks to avoid, rendering the version of phenomenology this book will try to imagine under the label "folk phenomenology." In others words, the *claim* is not important in itself (i.e., in its semantic or propositional content); the *ways* the claim is made are what matter most. Form, in this case, is content; accident is substance; the performance is the offering. Choosing not to make a claim *philosophically* is precisely the inversion that the two terms "folkloric reversal" refer to. This reversal is phenomenological in its movement away from aesthetics, a theory of art, and towards art itself—from theory towards practice, in order to enable and recover the practice of theory, the art of thought. The result will be a preliminary lens, introduced in the chapter to follow and then put into practice in relation to three things that are not easily divisible from each other or from anything else: education, study, and the human person. This is a trinity of sorts, another rendition of the endless "the one and the many" situations, where we find not one thing but three, not three but one. For instance, you and I, right here, together, writing and reading—*this* is education, study, and the human person. How could it be otherwise?

The *object* (first reduction), its way of *being* (second reduction), and its way of *being given* (third reduction) leave us with one final possibility: the offering, that which is prior to what is given and its logic of donation and duties of desert. In the sense of numerical succession, this is a fourth reduction. But the priority of the offering is not a fourth reduction in relation to the progression of the previous three. No. Unlike the previous phenomenological reductions, this is a simpler and less systematic *reversal*, interrupting the phenomenological progression, offering what it may be unable to give and what may never be received, but what is sufficient all the same.

THE OFFERING

This is precisely what art is and does that aesthetics cannot be or do: an offering. This is what the lover who offers yet never gives nor receives love understands: *Every thing that shows, offers.*[4]

Before the showing, the offering is the only condition of beauty, the condition for the possibility of what is shown. The folkloric reversal is an

---

4. This is a riff on Jean-Luc Marion's condition of givenness, "Everything that shows itself, offers itself," taken from my notes of his 2008 plenary address at the Franciscan University of Steubenville Conference on Christian Philosophy, titled "The History of Givenness."

attempt to find not what is first or last but what is *real*, with the credibility that art has when it speaks for and from itself. The beautiful is not an axiomatic or critical affair: it is simply the struggle to show what has been offered, with a hope that never carries the expectation of a gift. I recognize this voice as a practicing artist, a musician, a writer, and a teacher. It is this same voice that offers itself to and from phenomenology that might possess something worthwhile to show us as we move ahead into a new century, the century after the death of God and Man.

These historical deaths reveal a crisis of authority, yes, but also an anxious crisis. It is not so much the absence of a monarch, but, instead, the *mood* that ensues in the absence of authority. What will happen? Who will replace it? Philanthropy? Democracy? Transnational corporations, too big to fail, too small to believe in? In the previous century, one institution emerged as the favorite to remedy this social predicament: the school, in various formulations and models, some compulsory, others voluntary. Soon, an ideology of Education became the creed of that institution, and many today think that this is the only way forward. ("Education is your only way," says a mentor to an impressionable Mexican high school student at Baylor University in 1999.)

In this book, I will try as best I am able to describe education in its bare, vexing, and vast reality, along with other realities like study and the human person, held in symmetrical relation to a theoretical lens that, hopefully, will extend well beyond these pages, into better and more careful future work. This is not meant to ignore the schools of today completely. Inside these schools—and outside of them, too—there are people, real people, women and men of flesh and bone, and an endangered species of the human person: the teacher.

From the shaman to the rabbi, from the prophetess to the pedagogue, from imam to priest, from parent to professor: teaching is the art of showing. And showing is made possible by the offering. The teacher never knows for certain that the offering is given; the exchange is never clear or realized. The teacher can only be present, which is the first and last pedagogical offering, with the hope of showing something real, a hope without expectation or confirmation. When the offering is shown, beauty is present. When a lesson or a homily or a routine or a scale is complete, these are the only questions left to ask: What was offered? What was shown?

When a teacher is present, when there is being in love, even death is powerless in the face and eye of the offering. In this way, teaching is an answer and a story even more powerful and enduring than Genesis or the big bang. It is a folk story and song of art offered.

FOLK PHENOMENOLOGY

This book, then, is perhaps best understood as a meditation on teaching in an age when the teacher has again become an outcast, through the impossible attempt to teach under a new name for what is really nothing new at all: folk phenomenology, a way to imagine the real, gleaned from pages and experiences and ideas, but most of all from persons, wrestled together through the art of writing and editing. It is offered as a teacher who feels the anxiety of these times and also the joy, in the only way the offering is ever made: in love, in love, in love, with all the tragedy and life that love brings.

Two

I Am Not a Goose

Probably a crab would be filled with a sense of personal outrage if it could hear us class it without ado as a crustacean, and thus dispose of it. "I am no such thing," it would say …

WILLIAM JAMES, *THE VARIETIES OF RELIGIOUS EXPERIENCE*

INTRODUCTION

MY ELDEST SON INSISTS that he is not a goose. When I call him a "silly goose," he gets angry and indignant and scolds me, exclaiming, "I am not a goose!" At the age of three, he has a real interest in who he is and what he is not. He protests when referred to as something that, he believes, describes him as other than who he is. Along with not being called a goose, my son has made it clear to me that he is not to be called a variety of other things: a baby, a "little boy," other titles reserved for his younger brother, and any terms that describe him as anything less than a "big boy" or his name, *Tomas*. Not Tom or Tommy—and certainly not Bill. My son has a fierce and consistent passion to not be confused with being otherwise than who and what he is sure that he is.

If I wanted to be cruel to him, I could call him a goose, again and again, against his wishes. I could verbally torture him by repeating the word *goose* over and over—"Goose! Goose! Goose! Goose! Goose! Goose!" This gratuitous form of teasing would surely be child abuse. It would bring my son to tears and tantrums, causing him pain and suffering. If I persisted in doing this throughout his life, this sort of speech could lead to all sorts of trauma, the development of pathologies and emotional wounds. Ultimately, I could disfigure him into confusing himself with something other than who he is. A violation. Alienation. Even if he does not fully or partially realize it, this is at least part of why not being a goose is no small matter for Tomas. This is also why I cannot take it lightly. Asserting that he is not a goose is not a joking matter. This is not funny or cute. It is serious to him for reasons he seems to understand, even as he does not fully know them. He is prepared to yell, scream, cry, and even become violent, in order to resist the very idea, captured in a spoken word, of being such a thing. My son will fight against being called what he is not. At three years old he has a passion to be, live, and exist in a very particular kind of way: *not as a goose*. These desires will surely change throughout his life in their particular manifestations, but this general desirous condition will not. There is something primitive and beautiful at the root of his childish resistance that will endure and remain, something I not only see in him, but can find within others and myself. Even if it fades, it will never be totally absent. If it were to erode to the point of invisibility, it would be a great, disorienting harm. This negative response—"I am *not* a goose!"—is fundamental for Tomas, and it leads me to believe that it is also an absolutely real and nontrivial aspect of the human condition. It is something human persons have in common, can recognize in each other, and in other persons, too, especially within ourselves. If this is true—and I think it must be at least partially true—then it may also be a way to encounter and understand things, to describe what they are and what they are not.

In this chapter, I will continue using this example, along with several others, to introduce some of the key elements of this book. First, I will introduce three categories that, together, form a "trinitarian lens," a conceptual instrument I fashioned to carry out and organize this work. Second, I will elaborate on how and why ontology is most vividly and consistently revealed in our passions and erotic life. (What I mean by the terms "erotic" and "eros" is a singular, eternal, and irreducible desire for love: the love of love, the desire for desire, the mad longing for longing, passion for passion itself.) Third, after considering some objections, I will begin to show why these ideas require phenomenological methods of inquiry by noting some of the convergences and differences between scientific and phenomenological forms of knowledge. Here I will also address certain postmodern critiques of phenomenology and distinguish between the intertwined purposes of philosophy and phenomenology. Finally, I will set the terrain for the chapters to come through a discussion of the subject of imitation, and cite the enormous influence of the life and thought of William James on this work.

The main concern and purpose of this chapter is to provide the orientation necessary to embark on three descriptions (of education, study, and the human person) in the chapters to follow. Hopefully they will provide some insight into the enormous task of being within Being, living, and existing by seeking, sensing, and seeing with a fierce and radical fidelity to the absolute reality of our most profound desire: our desire for love and *theosis*, the desire for Desire, a desire that begins *in media res*, to be sure, always already—including our desire to not be otherwise—but a desire that cannot be pushed aside or replaced with other things willy-nilly. This is the erotic, desirous core of this project, embodied in the protest of my three-year-old son. He *showed* me this desire; I will try to *say* something about it.

THE CATEGORIES

What is real? This question cannot be answered outright as a generic query, but perhaps we can find some strategies or methods with which to explore it in a more concrete and subtle way. This impossible question is a very general way to begin to understand the scope of this study. A more specific approach would be not to ask what reality is in the abstract, but, instead, to ask what that thing over there is. What is *that*? But how does one identify *that* thing as real? Surely, pointing at this or that thing is not enough. This is the purpose of the categories of Being, subsistence, and existence. I hope to use them together as a conceptual lens, a tool for the imagination, a way to picture the real and to identify real things in a specific conceptual place or situation. This will add nothing to reality from the outside, but it will create a sense of its internal order and dimension by adding a few operationalized terms and governing concepts that may be useful for imagining and describing the real.

Here are some preliminary, basic senses of what each category describes and contains:

Being is the widest category of things. In order to be something instead of nothing, a thing must *be within* something. There is an antecedent something that sits behind everything. There is nothing outside of everything. Things must dwell within the context of Being in order to be things in the first and last place. Everything we assume to be a thing, then, must be what it is within the sphere of Being. This category describes the context within which all things are, where things subsist and exist. Anything outside of Being is nothing and therefore of no concern to us.

Subsistence[1] is the vital, energetic, and conceptual, as opposed to perceptual, category of things that are within Being, do not necessarily exist, and are nonetheless real. The force of gravity, for instance, subsists but does not exist. After all, force is not the exact same thing as matter. The presence of my now deceased grandfathers that I feel every day in love and memory may not exist, but it can and does subsist. The past and the future subsist, too. Who has seen time? No one. Yet no one can credibly deny its reality. Time subsists, too. In this category we find immaterial realities: concepts, forces, and energies.

Existence is the category of things within Being that subsist and that possess these two qualities (being within Being and subsisting), with the added feature of existing. In this category we find embodied, incarnate, and material things. For example, my fingers and toes are existing things in the present.

I will restate the categories in a slightly different way. Each category contains and pictures an aspect of the real. "Being" is a word that refers to the context for everything that is; everything that is real is contained within the referent of this term. "Subsistence" is a word that refers to the forces and energies that are within Being, but do not exist in a material or embodied way. "Existence" is a word that refers to the embodied and perceptual things we find within Being that also subsist, and exist in a particular, incarnate way.[2] These are operationalized terms, words used to create an accurate idea about things in any given situation or place. Together they form the dimensions for a conceptual picture of any place, thing, or situation. If we

---

1. Since this term is uncommon, I would like to say a bit more about where it comes from and also note a source of inspiration for these categories. In Alexius Meinong's "Theory of Objects," he, too, proposes an ontological model: existence, subsistence, non-existence, and non-subsistence. In the end, however, he determines that all the objects in these categories at least have "quasi-being." This began a long and interesting dispute between Meinong and Bertrand Russell. I have proposed my own categories not as a way to mediate in their dispute, but as a way to expand what I see as some of the analytic limits to Meinong's original metaphysical model.

2. For more on the distinction between concept and percept, see chapters 4, 5, and 6 of William James's *Some Problems of Philosophy*.

have a clear and imaginative sense of this picture, we can find these categories in all possible sites of reality, even within the ever-present structure of
desire. In other words, these categories also provide a sketch of our fundamental desires: the desire to be within and seek Being, the desire to survive
and live among the forces and tides of subsistence and sense them more
deeply, intimately, and presently, and the desire to exist and see and touch
the incarnate body and matter at hand. When we *see* anything perceptual
and material that exists, we also *sense* its subsistent forces and energies and
can *seek* what larger, all-encompassing Thing these things are within.

Imagine the popular image of an apple falling on Isaac Newton's head
as he rests under an apple tree. There are three basic things in this picture.
Each thing aligns symmetrically within the ontological categories, individually and as a whole. The first is the canvas that the whole event takes place
on, its context and world. This is what the capitalized term "Being" refers
to. The second are the ghost-like, invisible, and animating forces that are
related to the falling apple: gravity. These would be subsistence. The third
is the material apple that collides with Newton's material body, his head.
This would be existence. As you can imagine, this example is not strictly
metaphorical. It can be used allegorically, but it is rooted in a simple and
grounded analogy. These images do not *mean* anything; they simply are
what they are, and their being what they are confronts us with a structure
and order of things. The same basic analysis can readily be extended to any
site of reality.

When this picture is spatialized, a progression and harmony emerge
that describe the relationship between the individual categories, creating
what I will call them together: a trinitarian lens.

A TRINITARIAN LENS

Together, these categories locate and describe an elementary ontological
description that is pre- and proto-linguistic. As a whole, this lens shows
what William James called the "*Vorgefundenes* (the-thing-that-has-been-
there-before), which we cannot burrow under, explain or get behind." The
categories also yield a tool: a trinitarian lens, an eye of sorts, a conceptual
technology through which we can begin to seek Being, sense subsistence,
and see existence with fidelity to the reality of things and their inner order. Seeking, sensing, and seeing in this way, using this ontologically ordered lens, is the simplest way to understand the thinking that informs

the experimental and speculative approach for the ideas in this book. As any writer or musician knows, words that refer to the sense of sight are not about seeing through exclusively physical eyes; it is about seeing with the eyes of the mind and the heart, the eyes that can hear, smell, touch, and transcend. Vision in this case is not to be anatomized.

a trinitarian lens

The purpose of the trinitarian lens I have presented is to use the categories together, as a single and irreducible whole but in different focuses, in order to seek Being, sense subsistence, and see existence. This trinitarian lens, then, is itself a way of seeking Being, sensing what life forces are there, within it, and seeing the flesh of the matter. The more radical task and challenge is to live and act with harmony and fidelity to that trinitarian reality, but that task cannot be done without taking seriously the rigor of imagining it. Phenomenology is nothing more or less than a way to imagine the real.

The preliminary importance of the trinitarian lens of Being, subsistence, and existence can be asserted in the following ways. By looking at how each category impresses something real, we can see that each relates to the opening erotic condition expressed by my son's refusal to be called a goose:

> Being is important in the first place because I desire to be within something larger than myself and, insofar as I am within something larger than myself, I desire it. This first importance requires us to not only begin to take being within Being seriously at the front end of our conscious experience, but also to consider its total sufficiency across the plane of reality. There is nothing to add to it and all subtractions from it are contingent to it. Even reaching beyond the intentional aspects of volition and questions of mind and psychology: being within Being is sufficient. It is enough. It is more than human, more than life; it is beyond judgment or analysis. It is a mystery.

The importance of subsistence is that, since I must be within Being to begin and end with, then, I also desire to *survive* Being. To be alive within it. To be within Being has a vitalist impulse I feel within the order of subsistence. This begins to sense the worldliness of Being through the subsistent forces that inspire and sustain our vitality, but remain faceless and ghostly all the same.

The second leads to the third: existence. The desire for a face and a body, the desire to exist in a particularly concrete, embodied, perceptual, and human kind of way. In the flesh, incarnate; a human person of flesh and bone. As a human person I cannot merely subsist without a body, as a ghost, or with indifference to my flesh as a worm. I must exist. This third level of importance requires us to consider the unique sufficiency of existence: insofar as I am within Being, it is enough to exist, so long as that existence is within Being and among the invisible forces of subsistence. There is mystery in the completeness, the wholeness, the magnitude of existence, despite its apparent contingency and obvious mortality.

The importance of Being, subsistence, and existence provides us with a single, multiplex, trinitarian lens to organize our way towards seeking, sensing, and seeing things as they are, holistically. This wholeness, this completeness, this ontological ecology, is best described as beautiful and, based on that beauty, real. This is not a qualitative or axiomatic beauty nor it is an aesthetic provocation; it is simply that which shows itself in the offering, revealing the rigor of the trinitarian lens: attunement, balance, and grace. The way of using the lens can be further understood in its relationship to, and identity as, phenomenology,[3] rooted in the ontological passions, as displayed by my son's protest, "I am not a goose."

ONTOLOGICAL PASSIONS

The reason that not being a goose is a serious matter for my son is recognizable to me and real to him because of this common, erotic passion we share. It is an atomic reality, different in its manifestations, but identical in its desirous condition. These passions are not mere taste or personal fancies, they are *ontological* passions, which is simply to say that they play a constitutive role in our lives and originate from a condition that itself is erotic. The ontological passions to exist, to live, and to be within Being, then, are not rare. They seem to be at the root of everything: the biological survival of species and ecosystems, the emotional whimsy of lovers, the mysterious balance of the cosmos, the human obsession with gods and immortality, and more. At the very least, they are *less* than language. They are "less than" because they are simpler than verbal or symbolic identity and hermeneutic representations. They are more basic than words and their meanings. Words and symbols are derivative traces of the ontological passions.

Ontological passions, then, are less than the matter of what nomenclature seems to fit them best. To not be a goose is not principally about a name. The eros that drives the project of becoming, living, and existing works behind the scope of interpretation. In other words, *being is not the same thing as meaning.* There is difference between what something is and what something means. Ontology, the study of being, is not the same thing as epistemology, the study of knowledge. (And, as we will see later on in

---

3. Two texts that treat phenomenology in the ways that I am sympathetic to are both dedicated to its relevance to psychology. One is somewhat dated and the other is very recent: T. W. Wann, ed., *Behaviorism and Phenomenology* and Amedeo Giorgi, *Descriptive Phenomenological Method in Psychology*. The second and newer one is especially good.

this chapter, *knowing* is not the same as *knowing-about*.) The latter can only become the case if the former preempts it. Interpretation and meaning-making may be the task before us now as I write and you read, but hovering over, around, and inside us, unmoved by these word-markings and their grammatical order and corresponding references, are the ontological passions and the erotic realities they are wedded to. Ontology is the lesser, simpler, and therefore most fundamental dimension of things, most evident in the yearning to love and be loved, the desire to desire, nostalgia for nostalgia, the desire for Desire itself: the suicidal narcissism of eros, the madness of eros for itself.

In my own life, there is an ongoing sense that I do not resist being called this or that word or name because I dislike the account, the call itself, or the symbolic grammar of the calling. The problem is not linguistic or semiotic, although it may appear to be so on the surface when I express it in speech or grammar. My demands and resistance are not about language. Instead, I resist because I intuit—or to put it another way, because I understand even while I may not know it—that *I am at stake within the call*. My very being, life, and body are at stake—Being, subsistence, and existence. I sense that somehow I am the thing in question. But I desire to desire first, before the name and before the call, before and after the demand or the refusal. I desire to not be otherwise. This is because I am a less-than-linguistic thing. I am an erotic person because eros is first and foremost ontological, and therefore must be more potent, fecund, and real than symbols, words, grammar, and the epistemological accounts they prescribe. Even if meaning melts away, eros will remain, silently, in the dark. To be this erotic thing, to feel these ontological passions, is not to merely be strong-willed or sensitive: there is more than brute power within the passion to be and to not be otherwise. Eros is potent and pregnant with viral fruit. Like a virus, too simple to be an organism or bacterium, untreatable by antibiotics, ontology is a simpler thing than epistemology. Ontology is like a simple non-organism that, in its viral simplicity, is potent enough to take over and infect the more complex organisms of the body. Ontology is not marked by its complexity. The simplicity and sufficiency of ontology conceals and yields its powerful potency. And, again like a virus, it cannot be cured outright. Therefore, the ontological passions, stemming from the root of eros, are more than the collective intentional and voluntary efforts of the will. We are not free from desire, even when we desire to be free. Desire is fundamental.

Before the bacteria of language, that complex epistemological organism, we find eros: the virus of fecund desire, the desire for desire. We are infected with it and this infection gives birth to reality, present, past, and potential. We desire the whole: to be within the context of Being, to live among energetic forces and the invisible, and to exist in a particular, embodied way—or, at least, not in *that* otherwise way. When an account of our self is at stake in the recognition of a name by naming, misnaming, or leaving nameless, we agree or resist to such a thing out of this erotic and potent desire to be and become within Being, to be alive and not dead, to be embodied and corporeal. This desire I refer to as "eros" begins with the simple fact that we desire to be something: *something instead of nothing.* Being always seems to win our favor over non-being. Everything that subsists and exists presupposes that something *is.* And the Being we dwell in is not some airy fantasy; it is alive and material. Eros, then, cannot be sterilized; at most we can lose our desire for desire, but the desire for Desire will remain in some form or another. Our most hidden and silent desires cannot be superficial and disposable. Even the most banal and mundane desires hide a deeper and more potent reality that gives way to the dark, pregnant womb of eros.

Ontological passions include all desires, grand and shallow and in-between, including the desires that bring out such an indignant reply from my son when he is called a goose, or from any person who is insulted by a kind of existence that she feels degraded by. Facing the threat of defacement, I will protest. Confronted by the threat of only subsisting—being alive without existing, like Ralph Ellison's *Invisible Man*—I may lose my desire to live at all. The zombie exists without subsisting, and brings about the apocalypse, a material deadness. The end of the world is never the end of Being, it is merely a change in what is to be found there. There is an erotic ecology of eternity and life and matter that must be sought, sensed, and seen, together and with the proper pitch and tuning.

A VAGUE OBJECTION AND A BAD JOKE

Imagine the most straightforward objection to the claims I have just made. Someone might simply tell me that I am wrong. This objection may seem weak, unsupported, and extremely vague (Wrong about *what?*) but it carries a ready-made proof that is potentially devastating to what I have written thus far. Since a person who argues that something is simple and elementary is usually also implying, as I happen to be doing, that the thing in question is obvious, like the warmth of the sun on a crisp autumn morning or the coolness of shade and a soft breeze on a hot summer afternoon, then, to deny the obviousness of what is said to be obvious poses a formidable refutation all on its own.

But the rebuttal itself is a blessing to the assertion it seeks to critique. The performance belies the content because it carries the very thing it is attempting to dismiss. That is to say that when we deny ontological claims as trivial or impossible nonsense, we raise important ontological questions and issues nonetheless.[4] We cannot pretend to opt out of Being and the rest, even if we went to the extreme of committing suicide. Much like the perverse irony that is hatred, where even as we hate most passionately we find ourselves in love with it—or, to put it another way, where I can only hate properly if I love to hate the thing I hate—I could admit to the fact that I most certainly am wrong in a certain superficial sense and still feel, all the same, that I *am* not wrong. After admitting to possible error or mistake, I might ask the following question to my interlocutor: "But who am I, or who do you think I am, really?" Which is to say, "Stop talking *about* me, or at me, in some heady fantasy. Speak *to* me, directly! Tell me who I am, at least roughly speaking. Who am I? Talk to *me*!" To elaborate this point a bit, a schoolyard joke comes to mind. The word "am" may be used in more than one way, but its gesture to the person reveals more than its usage.

As a school child, when someone would say something like, "I'm hungry," I would often reply with something like this: "Hi Hungry, I'm Sam. Very nice to meet you." Depending on the mood of this person I had suddenly renamed, my classmate might act confused, clarify what they meant, laugh at my joke, or get annoyed at my antics. Regardless of their response, the point is rather obvious. When people say that they *are* this or that subsistent symptom of existence—like being tired, cold, angry, or hungry—they are not being serious about who it is that they are, and to act otherwise could only be a joke, a joke that confuses the "what" for the "who."

When I say things like "I'm thirsty," I am not making ontological claims.[5] Instead, I am giving symptomatic descriptions about how it is that

4. The ontological import of these questions might be said to be true yet boring nonetheless. What is hard about this state of mind—boredom—is that it seems to think that it can go about without taking the ontological import of things into consideration, but the very act of existing proves the exact reverse. In other words, there are no exceptions to the ontological condition. It is fundamental and universal.

5. This remark may appear to rashly overlook the raw experience of thirst, hunger, or cold. However, there is nothing at odds between the two of them. The ugliness that it is

other things are going for me. I am speaking *about* me. On its own, there is very little of me in the details about me—being tired or awake, cold or hot, angry or happy, hungry or full, and the rest. As we will see in chapter 5, the self of a person is never entirely reducible to itself and much less to the brute properties of its temporal existence. The claim "I am thirsty" may be empirically true regarding my symptom of thirst and my subsistent need to survive. I may indeed experience real thirst. But this experience I am having lacks the power to speak to me as I am and desire to be, not to merely speak *about* me. I cannot risk confusing my immediate hunger with my ontological passions. If I were to become nothing more than hungry, I would become otherwise than who I am. The result would be ontological disfiguration.

In Spanish, it is the difference between the two expressions for "I am": *Soy* ("I am") and *estoy* ("I am," meaning that "I have").[6] *Soy* always speaks in an existential voice while *estoy* can only speak from experience and often speaks in term of "I have." "*Tengo hambre*" ("I have hunger") is a common way to say "*Estoy hambriento*" ("I am hungry"). For this reason, such a joke would be impossible in Spanish—"*Soy hambriento*" is a ridiculous expression! I was never able to jest with my classmates in Mexico in this way because the language offers no opportunity for confusing the difference between *what* I am ("I am hungry") and *who* I am ("I am not a goose!"). In Spanish, things are not so easily allowed to get out of focus in this instance. But speaking Spanish is not enough to seek, sense, and see things faithfully. Remember: there is more than language at stake.

Ontologically speaking, while positive assertions seem impossible, I can make negative claims like this one: Tomas is not a goose any more than my phantom critic could say that "I *am* a philosophical error," or than my classmates *were* the abstract, symptomatic experience of hunger. To say otherwise, one would have to be joking and, like my son Tomas, we might still object to the joke as not being funny at all or, perhaps, being quite

---

to die of thirst, starvation, or cold is a phenomenon where we find the person disfigured to a mere body, to flesh and bone, without the ability to desire more than that. Or, in the related occasions of ascetic practices such as fasting or physical feats of endurance, we find exactly the reverse: the vitality of the whole being of a person sought through deprecating acts that push the body beyond its limit. In both of these cases the fact remains that the symptoms of our experience are not existential and when we find ourselves stripped down to them alone—when we are thirsty, starving, or cold—we are literally dying, which is hardly an existential model of being alive.

6. The same grammatical relationship exists in the conjugated interrogative terms *¿estas?* and *¿eres?*

offensive—or even dangerous. The greatest danger would be the loss of the thing itself—the object of desire, the most radical loss being the desire for desire—in our lack of desire for it, our inability to sense it, and the blurred visions that are substituted for reality or deny the real altogether.

My son's indignation over being called a goose is precisely so because it is this kind of bad joke that distorts the erotic ontology we find in the passions that give rise to the categories I have outlined here. It takes him as he is in the present moment and declares *that* thing, Tomas the human person, to be something else, something altogether different, something abstract and therefore ridiculous, like a distant, irrelevant goose. Tomas demands that I return to *him* in the real presence that we share together and leave behind that unrelated stupid goose. He is asking for me to treat *him*, not his symptoms; his "who," not his "what." Lacking a cure and facing positive uncertainty, he is asking me to do more than settle for palliative or reactionary treatments. I cannot cure his desire, I can only recognize our shared infection, eros. He is asking me to do the impossible: to love him totally as he is, subsists, and exists, all at once. To do this, I cannot simply change my speech. I cannot learn a new language with better words. I cannot be nice. I must acquire new desires, new sensations, and new eyes—I must regain my oldest longings, dreams, and vision. I must have a focused desire for Tomas and for him alone, without losing the world in my attempt to focus on him. I must focus by expansion while looking closely. Only when I can begin to seek, sense, and see him in this way will I be able to love him—to understand who he is and be present to him.

When Tomas exclaims, "I am not a goose!" he is not merely telling me what he is not. He has more to teach me than a purely negative lesson. He is also instructing me on how to arrive at who it is that he is, even as he has yet to arrive there himself. He is teaching me that in order to seek, sense, and see him as he is, to know him as an ontological, erotic trinity, complete within context (Being), among life forces (subsistence) and a material body (existence), I cannot simply stop saying the wrong words or avoid looking at the wrong images. I must attempt to return to him, to what is real. This is no small task and I must admit, even as I type these words, that I doubt what, if anything, I have accomplished in this regard. However, there is no question that the challenge presented to me by my son is of the utmost and most grave importance. And this importance is not merely personal, experiential, or contextual. It is not important simply because he is my son and I am his father. It is not a mere symptom of our shared genealogy. More than that, it underscores the erotic importance of ontology in general and the trinitarian lens offered here as a way of seeking, sensing, and seeing things as they are.

SEEK, SENSE, AND SEE

Through this tripartite structure of things, we can understand more clearly why we often behave like my three-year-old son. He has almost no positive ideas of who he is. For instance, he has little understanding of the significance of sexuality or gender, and often pretends to be a snowshoe hare or a manatee. Nonetheless, he has strong negative feelings about what he is called when addressed as a goose. He has yet to consider the forces that act on his life or the exact conceptual meaning of the words being used, yet he wants more than to merely survive, more than to merely be generically *there*, orphaned by indifference. He wants to exist, subsist, and to be within Being that is all but absent to him. Tomas has all these desires even as he lacks the insight to say what he is in any positive or comprehensive fashion. So too it seems with us. Even when we cannot express or know the exact terms of our being within Being, subsistence, and existence through positive ontological descriptions, we are still willing to defend ourselves against that which we feel that we are not. We resist whatever seems to trivialize who we are into something that is otherwise. This is an erotic resistance.

I am not a goose! I am not a spic! I am not a racist! I am not a resource! I am not an object! I am not your possession! I am not a human! In all these cases and many more, when threatened by the real possibility of existing as something we think that we are not, we find ourselves in proximity to the most violent kind of abuse and oppression: ontological disfiguration. This goes beyond the insult to identity, it threatens the very being of the world itself. If I am otherwise than what is real, then the problem is not my own, pure and simple. The problem extends beyond myself and into the realm of the real itself. The effect, however, is affective. The terms that change and distort are often our own desires and intuitions. The fundamentality of eros does not change the flux of emotions and deception, especially self-deception.

The route to this understanding is almost always negative. It becomes most clear when it is absent, and the rigor of the negative route is, perhaps, our best approach to understanding it.

This negativity is not limited to the realm of ontological passions. We can find a parallel to medicine that might enhance the images of viruses, infections, and cures. Consider the example of cancer. Cancer is neither a bacterium nor a virus proper (although it is sometimes referred to as "viral") and is treated very much like the ontological passions. We have nothing positive to say about it. By definition, we can offer no cure for an incurable disease like cancer. But we do seem to have strong negative advice available, tips on what *not* to do. Preventive guesses. Don't smoke. The only counsel we might have to offer to someone diagnosed with cancer can also only be negative since it would be unrelated to cancer proper, in the strictest sense. These negative suggestions are usually preventive and not meant to address the existing cancerous cells themselves. For instance, they may be palliative treatments that have nothing to do with curing the disease. Or there may be no suggestions, having more to do with suffering it, such as not treating it at all. There are also highly aggressive, but still indirect, treatments like chemotherapy. In these cases it is well-known that we cannot treat the existing cancerous cell as a *particular* thing in this way, we can only locate the general location and use radiation that generically kills just about anything. The most aggressive form of this negative "treatment," is, of course, amputation.

Because of the elusive—perhaps "impossible" is a better word—nature of certainty, we can be quite wrong and confused about cancer. How does it do what it does? What is it? In a similar way, we are often tricked into thinking things are something they are not—especially when that thing is myself—and we are left meandering through a series of indirect and palliative prescriptions. We can be misdiagnosed, too: left to subsist in a state of vegetative consciousness where our senses are unreliable, or even unavailable to us. But the point here is not to verify or falsify a positively true or untrue thing or self, or a singular and universal metaphysics or identity. Finding a positive cure is beyond the realm of this study. As I said before, this is *less* than the extravagant politics of identity and recognition and their palliative, and sometimes aggressive, hermeneutic treatments. To find this lesser phenomenon, we must excavate behind those politics and that language. We must even be willing to excavate behind meaning and locate the meaningless origin of Being. We must try to find the virus, directly and concretely as it is, even as uncertainty is our only certainty.

In order to do this, we will be required to begin with the earlier, more elementary phenomenon of eros. With time and rigor, this might bring us to the later mysteries of comprehensive metaphysics, selfhood, identity, and their politics of recognition and systems of ethics, aesthetics, and so on. But I doubt it. Regardless, when we focus on this earlier, lesser phenomenon we see that it is quintessentially and unavoidably ontological as opposed to hermeneutic. Eros does not submit itself to interpretation. It is a question of being as opposed to meaning, even as meaning reveals aspects of being through our senses and the disclosure of interpretive exercises such as reading and deciphering this sentence. What is this phenomenon? It is the desire to be within Being, to subsist, and to exist. The ontological passions. These desires can be described in many ways (biological, physiological, psychological, psychoanalytic, ethical, religious, political, aesthetic, and more), but they are first and foremost ontological. They raise the question of being within Being, subsisting, and existing. For human persons, it might raise the Heideggerian question of *Dasein*, which for Martin Heidegger meant the particularly human way of being a human person. *Dasein* attempts to capture all three senses of desire—being (*Sein*), subsistence (*Bestand*), and existence (*Existenz*)—all-at-once for the human person.

The negative objections we make—I am not a goose!—point to a lack of sight and focus. Anyone who seeks to recover a sense of the undisclosed positive thing that we cannot imagine or name must do more than offer categories. She must begin to arrange those categories in a way that can be put to use in the pursuit of sensation and vision. The hand reaches out in the dark, touching and feeling, using this sensation to see what matter is there. This study, then, begins and ends with the need to seek, sense, and see something as it is—or, at least, not as it is not.

EXCESS, KNOWING, AND REDUCTION

One of the richest articulations of what the term "phenomenology" refers to can be found in Heidegger:

> Thus the term "phenomenology" expresses a maxim which can be formulated as "To the things themselves!" It is opposed to all free-floating constructions and accidental findings; it is opposed to taking over any conceptions which only seem to have been demonstrated; it is opposed to those pseudo-questions which parade themselves as "problems," often for generations at a time.[7]

7. Heidegger, *Being and Time*, 50.

Thus we find the particular affinity between phenomenology and ontology. This relationship exists in stark contrast to other methods and approaches that respond to "problems." Phenomenology is about phenomena, a specialized word for things that appear. Again, Heidegger is very illuminating on this point when he highlights the "existential analytic" as it confines itself to the "ontological question." He writes:

> We must show that those investigations and formulations of the question which have been aimed at Dasein heretofore, have missed the real *philosophical* problem (notwithstanding their objective fertility), and that as long as they persist in missing it, they have no right to claim that they can accomplish that for which they are basically striving. In distinguishing the existential analytic from anthropology, psychology, and biology, we shall confine ourselves to what is in principle the ontological question.

He goes on to say—regarding science:

> Our distinctions will necessarily be inadequate from the standpoint of "scientific theory" simply because the scientific structure of the above-mentioned disciplines (not yet, indeed, the "scientific attitude" of those who work to advance them) is not today thoroughly questionable and needs to be attacked in new ways which must have their source in ontological problematics.[8]

As with scientific methods,[9] phenomenological method is rooted in a certain rudimentary empiricism. It does not, indeed cannot, say what is beyond the horizon of the embodied world. Unlike scientific methods, however, phenomenological method does not take the *immediate* world, the existential world of immediate sensation, as the sum total of what can be analyzed empirically,[10] nor does it find its finality or ultimate expression

8. Ibid., 71.

9. The methods of modern-day science vary a great deal across disciplines and orientations. To further complicate the matter, the meanings of scientific methods across history are inclusive to almost every form of inquiry. (As noted in chapter 1, the Middle Ages, *theology* was considered the queen of sciences.) So, what I mean by the term has more to do with the impact of these so-called "methods" that is much more obvious than the methods themselves. For example, while a statistician will almost never claim "causality" from her methods of quantitative investigation, the resulting impact of these studies frequently suggests an authority that is "research-based" or "scientific," revealing the methodological narrowness of science and the monopoly it claims in Education and modern society at large.

10. This is why William James's "radical empiricism" is very different from the

in mathematical logic.[11] Phenomenology can also attempt to analyze sub-sistent things like joy and even the phenomenon of Being itself.

Furthermore, phenomenological method does not take the horizon of immediate experience—or of the "scientific"—as the limit of ontological possibility. There is always more. There is always an excess of Being.[12] This "excess" is different from scientific "unknowns" because excess is ontological and sufficient, while the scientifically "unknown" is epistemologically insuf-ficient and something to be known. What "excess" is can be easily under-stood through any simple experiment of saturation. Consider this example that illustrates, in a very limited and preliminary way, what "excess" is.

Imagine doing this: take a large sponge (about twice the size of an adult hand) and dip it completely into the sea. Once it has absorbed its limit and has been utterly saturated, remove it. When the sponge is removed, take careful notice about how this completely-saturated sponge behaves: when it is lifted from the sea, loaded with water, it does not merely "drip" with extra droplets of water, it gushes with the excess of the sea.[13] What takes place in this example is excess: Being is the sea, and we are within it, pulled by the subsistent tides and forces, existing as an embodied sponge, always gush-ing with excess—saturated with and within Being, alive with energy and spirit. To paraphrase the Psalmist: *Our existential cup overfloweth with and within Being.* Therefore, unlike the methods of science, phenomenologi-cal method is not intended to simply address the cup of existence as fully

---

empiricism of science, or what he calls "medical materialism" in his *Varieties of Religious Experience*: it addresses experience in its widest sense.

11. In the preface to *Ressentiment*, Max Scheler makes this same distinction between scientific and phenomenological method very clearly. He writes: "It is one thing to sift the data of inner observation and to set them up as compounds, then to decompose these into ultimate 'simple' observation and experiment, the conditions and results of such combinations. It is quite another to describe and understand the units of experience and meaning which are contained in the totality of man's life itself and have not merely been created by an artificial process of 'division' and 'synthesis.' The first method, influenced by the natural sciences, is that of a synthetic-constructive psychology which wants to *explain*. The second method characterizes an analytic and descriptive psychology which wants to *understand*" (19).

12. The excess of Being, for Marion, is what leads to the "saturated phenomenon" and anchors the theological turn in his rendition of a phenomenology of givenness. See Marion, *In Excess.*

13. Another way to think of saturation would be by considering the reverse: the drop-let of water that can be absorbed fully by a sponge. This is the reverse of excess. It also brings to mind the impossibility for an existential sponge to dip into the sea and literally take it all into itself, leaving nothing behind.

as possible. The phenomenologist tries—and always must fail—to explore the very horizon of saturation and gain insight into the ontological excess that eludes our particular ways of being-within, subsisting, and existing, thereby extending potentiality, the saturation-point of the imaginable, the possible, and the real.[14]

Another limited example is the difference between analog and digital photography or electric instrumentation. The analog picture, developed with light and tint and heat, is literally more saturated with things—shapes and colors—than the digital picture, captured in electrons and pixels. The mark of fidelity is the highest saturation point, which ultimately is the thing itself.

Also unlike scientific methods, phenomenological method does not exclusively seek out the epistemic knowledge that we find in Aristotelian categories or elsewhere.[15] Most importantly, phenomenological method does not "know" in the ways that we are accustomed to "knowing-about" in the modern age of the dominance and autarky of scientific rationality. As we have seen (in my earlier point concerning language), the kind of knowledge offered through phenomenological method is *less* extravagant, and therefore more potent and infectious, than epistemological knowledge. Phenomenological knowledge is itself ontological: it is a way of knowing Being, subsistence, and existence that, in turn, is a way of being-within Being, subsisting, and existing. In the end, it disappears as knowledge and becomes something like understanding, something you can understand without knowing. Love.

After all, the desire to know is never properly epistemological, pure and simple. To desire the fulfillment of the Socratic dictum is not to be interested in knowing *about* one's self. Less than that, it is to "know thyself." In this way, epistemology is always too advanced, and therefore less fundamental, for ontology. It only appears later as a complex organism—like symbols and languages and their meanings—infected and fitted with eros,

14. There is no good reason that I can think of that explains why a scientist cannot observe excess. But this would not be a product of the scientific method; it would be from an intuition or a daydream. Whenever science explodes the limits of the empirical—like Newton and Einstein—the credit cannot properly be given to "science" per se, but, instead, to imagination. In this way, science is most impressive when the scientist becomes a phenomenologist—especially in physics and psychology. This phenomenological nature of movements or shifts in science is verified in the view held by Thomas Kuhn in his authoritative *Structure of Scientific Revolutions* that amounts to something like this: science is itself immune to science.

15. Aristotle, *Nicomachean Ethics*, 424.

but oftentimes ignorant or forgetful of the fecundity of that desire. (As I will continue to point out: this fecundity is a hallmark of this particular sense of eros.) Epistemology too often loses eyes for itself and becomes sterile. For this reason, one might even go as far as to suggest that epistemology is not epistemological. There can only be knowledge-about something after there has *been* something (within Being) and it has become something that tells us things we consider to be knowledge-about it. It can only be about something after it has been (within Being), born from the vast womb of eros. Even after this *is-ing*, there are still further distinctions between types of knowledge that show the limits of what we are doing when we presume to know. Unfortunately, again, the English language is ill suited to explain this point. In order to do so, please consider the difference between the two words for "knowing" in Spanish: *saber* and *conocer*.[16]

If someone were to ask me, "*¿Oye Samuel, sabes donde esta la farmacia?*" (Hey Sam, do you know (*saber*) where the pharmacy is?), my reply might reveal that I do know-about (*saber*) where it is (*Sí, yo se esta la farmacia*), but my *saber* knowing is only *about* the pharmacy. On the other hand, if someone were to ask me "*¿Dime Samuel, conoces este niño?*" (Tell me Sam, do you know [*conocer*] this child?), my reply might reveal that while I might know-about (*saber*) the child (what she looks like, what color her hair is), I do not know (*conocer*) her. Or, on the other hand, if the child is my youngest son, Gabriel, then I would exclaim that I do know (*conocer*) him: "*Si, claro que lo conozco. ¡Es mi hijo—Gabriel!*" (Yes, of course I know [*conocer*] him. He is my son—Gabriel!).

Here is a simpler linguistic example of the difference between these two ways of knowing: Take a standard salutation in Spanish like "*Mucho gusto conocerte.*" This literally means "Much pleasure to know (*conocer*) you." The less literal translation implies something more like the English formality, "It's a pleasure." This, of course, implies that it is a pleasure to know someone by meeting her now, in the flesh, not to merely hear or read about her or know-about (*saber*) her otherwise. Now, imagine the rudeness and absurdity in the substitution, "*Mucho gusto saberte.*" It is already poorly conjugated, but it also expresses a very different meaning: "Much pleasure to know-about (*saber*) you." This is clearly not what we mean by the English expression, "It's a pleasure." And for good reason! After all, the pleasure we get is presumably not from knowing-about (*saber*) people, but

16. In analytic philosophy, one can find similar veins of inquiry in Gilbert Ryle's distinction between "knowing how" and "knowing that" in *The Concept of Mind*.

from meeting them and knowing (*conocer*) them concretely—in the flesh. That is why, if I met someone famous, someone who I knew-about (*saber*) beforehand, I would still say that is a pleasure to know (*conocer*) them now, as opposed to merely having known-about (*saber*) them before.

Therefore, *saber* is a form of the verb "to know" that can only be used to speak of information or data: knowing *about* things. *Saber* never presents the chance, in any conjugated form, for substitution with its unrelated cousin, *conocer*: the knowledge of things themselves.[17] *Saber* is to know-about. *Conocer* is to know. *Knowing-about* is epistemological knowledge. *Knowing* is something that at least approaches ontological knowledge.[18] Sometimes, knowing-about is an opening move toward diving into the depths of knowledge and knowing to the point of complete saturation, ending in understanding or something even more bare and radical. Other times, knowing-about is confused with knowing and we forget what knowing is; we lose our senses and appetite for ontological knowledge, things go out of focus, and our vision is monopolized and distorted by knowing-about. Meaning becomes the horizon of Being. The trinitarian lens shares the phenomenological spirit in trying to seek after the desire to know without substituting it exclusively with knowing-about.

The distinction between epistemological and scientific knowing-about things and ontological and phenomenological knowing things themselves is not mutually exclusive. Nonetheless, there is an artistic dimension present in the ontological orientation of phenomenology that is often absent to epistemology and science, and absent by practical necessity. Take archery, for example: the sport and skill of shooting an arrow from a bow at a target. While the act may seem generic, there are two very different ways to shoot an arrow from a bow at a target. Using the modern compound bow, the archer is a scientist who makes calculations and sets her sight on the target while squinting down the shaft of the arrow in relation to the target and the aiming mechanisms on the modern bow. Using a longbow, however, the archer simply has to acquire the intuitive ability, through practice and repetition, to *feel* where the arrow is going in relation to the full context

17. There is also a colloquial usage of *conocer* that uses it as a pseudo-form of *saber* (e.g., *¿Conoces Argentina?* which is a way of asking, "Have you ever been to Argentina?"), but with the slightest clarification and attention to the direct object it becomes clear that this usage blends the two senses and treats the direct object like a subject predicated on knowing it in a way that goes beyond knowing about it.

18. From this point forward I will exclusively use these terms—knowing-about and knowing—to distinguish between the two types of knowledge.

of the shooting. This difference exists for a variety of reasons, beginning with the fact that modern bows hold the recoil at the back of the draw and longbows do not, but the greatest difference is that the practical method of aiming and shooting is fundamentally different. One is science and the other is art. One involves epistemic knowing-about and the other requires ontological knowing. Neither escapes the fundamental passions, but each approach makes different demands of rigor and fidelity.

A more common example is throwing a football or shooting a basketball. While there is a scientific knowing-about the physics of each set of motions and mechanics, there is another knowing that is the hallmark of the art of the sport, the one that is at use in the pressure of the game and is the most difficult to master. This is what is meant when a linebacker is said to "have a nose for the football" or a tennis player is said to "have a great feel for the game." The art of sporting, in effect, shows us that to know-about doing something is insufficient; we must know the thing in an intuitive way that transforms the act from science to art. And art always begets science; truth is born from beauty. This is because every form of art is a kind of constitution that is ontological and erotic through and through. We would rather have artists on our team than scientists—even in the sports played at an operating table or in a laboratory.

Return now to my son's objection. The positive challenge presented by my son to seek, sense, and see him, is to know him in exactly this artistic kind of way. To know him as a saturated ontological subject, not to know-about him as a dry epistemological object or datum. Tomas challenges me to know him as he is within Being, in the particular way he subsists and exists—not to merely know-about him. In order to know him in this way, as a practical approach, I, like the scientist, might begin with knowing-about. But I cannot end with it. I must move from knowing-about the child (what he looks like, what he prefers to eat, whether he is potty-trained or not, whether he is allergic to peanuts or not) and begin the impossible task of knowing him as he is, in excess. To *conocerlo*: literally, to know him. To stop settling for knowledge and begin to desire understanding.

So too with any phenomenological approach: Phenomenology seeks, again and again, to know things themselves[19] from their being within Being, to their subsistence, existence, or both. In this way we see that the trinitarian lens is a phenomenological instrument for knowing and understanding

---

19. Take careful notice that a "thing itself" is not the same thing as the Kantian "thing in itself."

things ontologically that by its very terms must reject the poverty of only knowing-about. Even if we begin and end knowing-about things, as I always seem to, phenomenology must remain restless for knowing and understanding, gazing again and again into the lens to find the impossible things we seek, sense, and see.

The ontological knowledge and understanding that might come from a prolonged and fruitful look into the trinitarian lens should also lead us to something different than purely "phenomenological" accounts of phenomena like those articulated by Edmund Husserl's "objects,"[20] Heidegger's "Being,"[21] or even Jean-Luc Marion's "givenness."[22] Heidegger himself says as much in his essay "My Way to Phenomenology," where he writes:

> But in what is most its own phenomenology is not a school. It is the possibility of thinking, at times changing and only thus persisting, of corresponding to the claim of what is thought. If phenomenology is thus experienced and retained, it can disappear as a designation in favor of the matter of thinking whose manifestness remains a mystery.[23]

In other words, the names and the tradition in general are too abstract to merit serious consideration as things for reduction (a term I will describe in the following paragraph). This is why I have focused on describing phenomenology itself as a thing, a process, an orientation and disposition to things, as best I know it, instead of reporting back to you what I know-about it. In fact, when I look at phenomenology through the trinitarian lens, I suspect that there is nothing properly or necessarily "phenomenological" about phenomena. Phenomena are things, appearances within Being that may subsist, exist, or both. We might even simply call them *stuff*. What is properly "phenomenological," then, is the practical approach, how phenomena are known through reduction. This is the positive imperative in my son's objection. He wishes for me to know him in a particular kind of way. And while he cannot tell me who that person he is *is*, what forces and energies drive his life, or in what particular embodied way he exists, he can guide me by teaching me how to look behind the complex symptoms and seek the impossible cure by paying close and careful attention, with tragic and faithful eyes for him as he is (within Being), not merely about-him—for

20. Husserl, *Essential Husserl*.

21. Heidegger, *Being and Time*.

22. Marion, *Being Given*.

23. Heidegger, *On Time and Being*, 82.

who he is, not only *what* he may be. In this way, phenomenology simply is a way of knowing and understanding, through a phenomenological reduction of seeking, sensing, and seeing whatever is the case.

We can understand the meaning of phenomenological "reduction" in a preliminary way by considering a culinary reduction. Taking its literal work as a way to seek, sense, and see things, we can understand what a "phenomenological reduction" does. A culinary reduction is the process where a liquid of some sort (usually a stock, sauce, or gravy) is simmered. This simmering allows certain parts of the liquid to evaporate, which has the effect of rendering a more intensely flavorful and rich substance, like a fig reduction. There is no doubt to the palate of anyone eating a fig that the reduction tastes "figly," although the flavor always exceeds our capacity to experience it completely, it saturates our sense of taste. The most radical reduction imaginable would simply disappear. In the same way, phenomenological reduction is how we go about knowing phenomena or things as best we can by taking them as they are and moving inward through a gentle caress (like evaporation) of the imagination to intensify them and render them more radically saturated as they are.

Phenomenological reduction, then, can be defined in this way: it is the practical way by which we apply the heat (alluding to the stove in the kitchen) or a bow (alluding to the violin in the concert hall) of our imagination's eye to a thing that, with time, rigor, and gentle balance—so as to try to avoid disfiguring it by burning it or going out of tune—renders it into a more robust and focused expression of itself. Ontological fidelity. And there is nothing certain or pure about this reduction. Imaginative sight and sensation sought through reduction is not meant to purify the thing itself, but simply to render it in a way that is more present and possible to its being within Being, subsistence, and existence. Concerning human persons, this more robust expression creates the distinct awareness of, and attention to, the total saturation of our embodied existence by subsistent forces, all within the context of Being. It gives us a trinitarian scent of a world of Being, ghostly life forces, and our flesh, fluids, and bones.

The essence of a reduction may not be its taste or sound at all; it may simply be the thing fully evaporated that leaves behind an unquestionable aroma of itself, like that sacred moment of silence at the end of a moving performance, just before the applause begins.[24] We know immediately what

---

24. Anyone who has heard a moving piece of music knows (*conocer*) that this silence is not a hypothesis. I will never forget the time I saw the solo bassist, Michael Manring,

it is, even though we may not know-about it. We understand. A beautiful smell is just that: something we know even though we may not know-about it at all. Silence that is utterly saturated with beauty is the same sort of thing. It simply *is* beautiful. Such is the ontological power of art. It is arresting on its own terms. And without this ontological scent or silence we cannot taste or hear properly, although we can still divide and consume calories into our stomach or sound waves into our ears. This essential scent and silence of ontology brings us to the question of metaphysics. Looming in this phenomenological thing to be known and understood lies a reasonable apprehension concerning that ancient and dangerous fruit: metaphysics and pure essentialism.

PLATONISM[25] AND POSTMODERNISM

I will not torture this point, because it ought to be fairly clear by now from my description of ontology and phenomenological method that the delayed metaphysics of folk phenomenology are of *this* world—the only world of time and space and the imagination—not a separate world of forms like the dwelling-place of the Platonic Demiurge. In this respect, scientific and phenomenological methods are cut from the same cloth: they both reject the distant correspondence theory of Platonic recollection and its otherworldly forms that are caged by temporality. Examining the self, for example, the phenomenologist cannot ignore the body as a measly cage of the soul any more than the biologist could do the same sort of thing. From this new, post-Platonic metaphysics is born a different ontological essence. Unlike the "pure essence" of Platonism, or even the Kantian "thing-in-itself," the essence of phenomenology is neither pure nor impure, but, instead, just the thing: a thing within Being that may subsist, exist, or both. This minimal thing is the

---

perform a double-bill at the Cedar Hall in Minneapolis with the Canadian fingerstyle guitarist, Don Ross. After performing one of his compositions, inspired by a Muslim call to prayer, the entire room did not applaud for at least twenty seconds. It was as if we were all in mourning for the beauty that just ended. That tragic silence was the essence that the song left behind, like a scent of home that is strongest when away or in the first moments of the return.

25. It is important not to confuse "Platonism" with Plato. I would regret to be read as using Plato as a foil for my argument here. I only want to bring up the well-known distinction between Platonic metaphysics and their fidelity to a correspondence theory of reality and the post-Platonic metaphysical views of modern philosophy that reject correspondence. The strongest argument against correspondence I can think of in philosophy is Richard Rorty's book *Philosophy and the Mirror of Nature*.

only possible purity to be found, and because of the excess of Being it inhabits (and is constituted by in turn), there is never the possibility of knowing with the metaphysical purity of Platonic—or scientific—certainty.

Let us return to the fig reduction. It may seem that its essence is singular and purely described by the object we associate with the noun. But, upon closer inspection and wider imagination, we find that even a fig reduction eludes a singular, purified articulation. What is a fig but a collection of flesh wrapped in skin, with seeds that lead to its stem that is a kind of branch that is a kind of trunk that is a kind of root that subsists on the nourishment of the fortunes of the earth, rain, and sun, all within the vast, intimate world of Being? And yet a fig reduction remains remarkably "figly." This is the paradox of phenomenological essentialism that is absent to Platonic essentialism.

This is not only a reply to the Platonist. It is also a reply to certain post-modern[26] antipathies for phenomenology that condemn it as fatally essentialistic—not unlike, if not the same thing as, the essentialism of Platonism. Most notable, of course, would be Michel Foucault's critique of Jean-Paul Sartre and others during the late sixties, the time when Foucault published what many consider to be his most abrasive dismissals of phenomenology: *The Order of Things* and *Archeology of Knowledge*.[27] When attending to these so-called dismissals it is important to note[28] that in-between the publication of those books he acknowledged the now popular problem of the subject in "What Is an Author?"[29] and, four years later, he continued to raise similar preoccupations in his preface to the English publication of *The Order of Things*. This phenomenological theme of the subject in Foucault is a now well-known notion that he continued to articulate until his untimely death in 1984, and is among the most prescient, and difficult, questions of Foucault scholars today.

---

26. It is well known that there is no single thing called "postmodernism" and that more complex and complicated articulations such as structuralism, post-structuralism, post-foundationalism, and more have perhaps surpassed it. I only use the term as a placeholder for all these names and traditions.

27. English translations include Michel Foucault, *The Order of Things* (New York: Random House, 1970), and Michel Foucault, *The Archaeology of Knowledge* (London: Routledge, 1972).

28. As I have in an essay review for *Foucault Studies*; see Samuel Rocha, review of *Remarks on Marx* and *Power*.

29. Foucault, *Language, Counter-Memory, Practice*, 113.

There are others who are frequently called "postmodern" who have even more direct ties to phenomenology. Consider the powerful work of Jacques Derrida. We cannot ignore his seminal contributions to the Age of the Post that grow directly out of his engagement with, and critique of, Husserlian phenomenology,[30] which led to his masterful work on language and the articulation of *différance* and *déconstruction*: those things of which anything said is surely incomplete. And while this work of his has garnered widespread attention, his lesser-known phenomenology of *le donné* (the gift) produced a rich disagreement with his former student, Jean-Luc Marion, on the phenomenology of donation and its ties, or lack thereof, to theology.[31] And, of course, there is the tremendous influence of Friedrich Nietzsche on both of these thinkers and others; an influence that may not be properly phenomenological but is at the very least proto-existential: alongside Kierkegaard's theistic existentialism, we find Nietzsche's atheistic version of what it means to *be* under the ontology we find within the "will to power."

For bibliographic thoroughness, we should also not forget the Heideggarian behemoth that is acknowledged by Foucault, Derrida, and so many others who are considered to be "postmodern"—including the self-described phenomenologist Marion whose phenomenological study of theology has given his work the title of "postmodern theology." In Heidegger's case, of course, the question is not whether he was a phenomenologist. That case is settled. It is more whether his Nazism discredits his phenomenology or not.[32] Furthermore, given the proliferation of ontological studies that have come out of—and have also, to a certain extent, abandoned—postmodernism, as with the "political ontology" we find in the popular works of Giorgio Agamben, Alain Badiou, and Slavoj Žižek, it seems that this much must be admitted: what many call "postmodernism" is littered with phenomenology.

For this reason, it seems that postmodern critics who would try to sever the tie between phenomenology and postmodernism do so rather carelessly, for these traditions are not two different things completely. They share a mixed—and, in many cases, exactly the same—genealogy.

30. See Lawlor, *Derrida and Husserl*.

31. See Robyn Horner's *Rethinking God as Gift: Marion, Derrida, and the Limits of Phenomenology*, which largely grew out of the famous debate between Derrida and Marion at Villanova in 1997 on the question of gift.

32. For a brief and moving analysis of this question, read Richard Rorty's straightforwardly titled chapter, "On Heidegger's Nazism," from his book *Philosophy and Social Hope*, 190–97.

According to that genealogy, we find this much to be historically probable in the present: to do away with the former would make the latter impossible. To be clear, let me repeat myself: By rejecting the essentialism of Platonism, phenomenology also rejects the rather caricatured critique posed by certain interpretations of postmodern thought, along with similarly skeptical views of ontology by positivism and vulgar articulations of pragmatism.

This is not to say that phenomenology is without fault or not in need of constant revision. It is neither to deny the disturbing essentialism of Husserl's transcendental phenomenology nor to look past the abuses of Nietzsche and Heidegger by the Third Reich and others. After all, phenomenology hardly proclaims a single gospel, and its controversies often frame the field more than its convergences.[33] It does seem meritorious to say that while the product of phenomenological reduction—a strange sort of essence I have described as eros—may be difficult to navigate and may even appear at times to be nothing more than a Platonic essence—after all, this is the critique of Husserl by Heidegger (and Derrida) and of Heidegger by Marion—the requisites of the actual phenomenological work are such that anything dualistic or other-worldly is nothing more than a fantasy or a mistake. Not unlike the goose that my son so abhors.

PHILOSOPHY AND PHENOMENOLOGY

Having discussed the converging genealogies of phenomenology and postmodernism, I should also briefly mention the genealogical relationship between philosophy in general and the philosophical moment of phenomenology. Since philosophy and phenomenology can be very opaque things, I will illustrate my point by referring to a peculiar culinary trend that I recently became aware of.

"Real food" has become trendy. This includes Paleo diets and kale. There are popular books on the subject,[34] growing attendance at farmers markets, and restaurants that boast that they serve such food to their patrons. I ate at one of these restaurants, a popular hamburger and fries eatery

---

33. See, for example, the controversies of French phenomenology after Emmanuel Levinas in application to theology in Janicaud et al., *Phenomenology and the "Theological Turn."*

34. And the ones written by Michael Pollan are worthwhile and highly accessible things to read. *The Omnivore's Dilemma, The Botany of Desire,* and his most recent, *In Defense of Food,* are all worthwhile books to read, in my estimation.

named Five Guys Burgers and Fries. It came highly recommended to me, and for good reason. It makes very good-tasting burgers and fries. What is the secret? It's simple. They use real food for the featured ingredients. Fresh, never frozen ground beef that is formed into hamburger patties by real hands; real potatoes that are cut into spears and fried in real oil; real peanuts that one can shell and eat while waiting for the food to be cooked to order; and so on. They even boast the name and geographic place of the farm that their potatoes and peanuts are shipped from on a chalkboard display. People seem to be very impressed by the novel idea of eating potatoes and peanuts that come from such a worldly origin, a real farm. Imagine that, using real meat and real potatoes to make hamburgers and French Fries. "Real food," what a revolutionary concept!

Satire aside, this is the world we live in: a world where worldliness has itself become a spectacle. We are amazed by the truly ordinary because we have mostly forgotten that it was there or never knew of it to begin with. In one sense, this is what some might call the human condition. I am not so sure that there ever was a time of authenticity. This is the lesson of Plato's cave that has been repeated across time in almost every philosophical movement. Philosophy has always been speaking to this perennial quest and longing for deep recovery. The Socratic practice of *philo-sophia*, love of wisdom, is tailored to address the human struggle to fulfill the deepest desires to be a human person: to be within Being, to live, and to exist. As Foucault put it, philosophy has always been invested in the "care of the self."

Foucault's Nietzschian genealogies also remind us that things have also changed. In recent historical times, there has been a heightened sense that this philosophical quest for selfhood, and for a sense of what is real, has come under uniquely modern threats. As early as Rousseau, and most famously in Marx, we find the notion of "alienation" that speaks not only to the human condition in general, but most presciently to the present, to the modern times in which we live. Therefore, philosophy and phenomenology are not entirely different from each other, although they do serve distinct purposes. Philosophy is powerful, but, like the wind, it seems to have a mind of its own. Philosophy goes on undisturbed by the tides of time, even before it existed in the form of a discipline or as anything at all. Unlike this perennialism of philosophy, phenomenology is not timeless. Phenomenology is not immune from history or politics. Phenomenology is impossible without the unique challenges of our time—especially in the globalizing

West during the previous century. Phenomenology is impossible without a genealogy that makes it necessary and prescient for the times we live in.

Similar to the basic difference between economics and socialism, where the exchange of capital is general and reactions against modern capitalism are specific, so too with philosophy and phenomenology: We cannot imagine ourselves without philosophical concerns and questions that are fundamental and timeless. We also cannot imagine phenomenology without the historical changes of the recent past and the predicaments of modernity. In response to the popularity of "real food," phenomenology comments on this contemporary historical obsession, while philosophy speaks to the basic fact that we grow hungry. In my view, we need both.

IMITATION

Now I would like to turn my attention to a recent book in the philosophy of education that is not explicitly phenomenological, but does articulate an important question in a way that leads me to believe that the subject matter is deeply infused with ontological preoccupations that might serve to make my own more clear. My hope is that it will serve as another way to articulate the curiosities I have invested in for this project. In his book, *Imitation and Education: A Philosophical Inquiry into Learning by Example*, Bryan Warnick asks this question: "How do we learn from the lives of others?"

While I find his reply interesting, I am most impressed with the phenomenological profundity and insight with which he poses the question, especially in his opening paragraph, which I find to be deeply inner-directed, perhaps psychoanalytic, and without a doubt psychological. He writes:

> My life has been a mirror of the lives around me. I find myself becoming like the people I am exposed to; I reproduce their actions and attitudes. Only rarely, however, can I recall making a conscious decision to imitate. One of my teachers was such a towering personality that he radically changed the direction of my life, though I was scarcely aware of his influence at the time. Only long after did I recognize his imprimatur emerging on everything from my occupational decisions, to my views about religion and politics, and even to my preferences about where to go to lunch. I seem to have been passive fuel awaiting his incendiary presence. When I think about his influence, I wonder how it occurred and whether it has, on the whole, been a good thing for me to have learned in this imitative way. *This book is, among other things, a personal attempt*

*to answer questions about how I became who I am. It is an attempt
to understand how one human life can sway another and to better*
comprehend the meaning and value of this influence.[35]

Here, Warnick declares his book as *being* two things: (1) "a personal
attempt to answer questions about how I became who I am . . ." and (2) "an
attempt to understand how one human life can sway another . . ." Under
this dual purpose, the question, "How do we learn from the lives of others?"
seems to verge on impropriety depending on what that question means.
What does this book have to do with "learning"? What does "learning"
have to do with becoming who one is and swaying another life? What does
he mean by "learning"?

The answer seems to vary according to the *saber/conocer* or knowing-
about/knowing distinction. If by "learning," Warnick means "learning-
about-things," then it seems to be altogether unrelated to what he states that
this book *is*. However, if by "learning" Warnick means "learning-about-
things" and "learning-things," or simply "learning-things," then he meets the
self-imposed, ontological prerequisites of his text. In other words, in order to
be faithful to what he declares his book to be, Warnick seems to suggest that
what is at stake in learning is not the epistemic knowledge—knowing-about
or *saber*—so often attributed to it, but, at least in addition to that, ontological
knowledge—knowing or *conocer*. And beyond that, understanding. A mere
case of epistemology like *saber*-learning cannot sustain the desires of the
author that constitute his book. Without ontological knowing, Warnick cannot accomplish what he is striving for. None of us can. On its own, epistemological knowing-about denies the fact that, first, all things must be-within
Being. This is how Heidegger put it in *Being and Time*:

> We must show that those investigations and formulations of
> the question which have been aimed at Dasein heretofore, have
> missed the real *philosophical* problem (notwithstanding their ob-
> jective fertility), and that as long as they persist in missing it, they
> have no right to claim that they can accomplish that which they
> are basically striving for. In distinguishing the existential analytic
> from anthropology, psychology, and biology, we shall confine our-
> selves to what is in principle the ontological question.[36]

We could imagine this Heideggarian objection being raised against
Warnick's book or, more generously, we could at least see this objection as

35. Warnick, *Imitation and Education*, 1–2 (emphasis mine).
36. Heidegger, *Being and Time*, 71 (italics in original).

a way to reorganize the thrust of the book. Both readings argue that the sentiment of the question that we find in Warnick's confessional introduction cannot be separated from the question itself. Learning cannot be a matter of epistemology, pure and simple. More than that, learning does not originate from epistemic knowledge, but, instead, from our desires and questions of Being, subsistence, and existence. Without eros, there is no learning. So, noting Warnick's phenomenological description of the ontology of his own study, I would like to pursue much of the same content—with many of the same haunting curiosities—with this phenomenological look at education, study, and the human person through the trinitarian lens I have described here.

OVERVIEW AND JAMES

I will organize my thoughts in the chapters to follow by following the categories of the trinitarian lens (Being, subsistence, and existence). In the chapter to follow, I will consider the question of education: the thing that is, or might be, education. My reply will be minimal. I will propose that education is a mystery in the positive sense: a real thing, not a negative absence or nothingness, not a subsistent energy, not a material object. In the fourth chapter, I will move from Being to subsistence in order to look at study as an erotic force as opposed to a purely volitional practice. In the fifth chapter, I will make some suggestions about the existence of the human person facing the unique challenges that threaten the ability to exist at all. In the sixth and final chapter, I will comment on the implications of using the trinitarian lens as a whole and a potent educational vision that might—and must—possess the fecundity to withstand and outlast the death of school. Each chapter is also written at a length that *shows* the relative symmetry between the different categories. This is as important as what it *says*.

For the sake of clarity, allow me to restate how the chapters to follow interact with the ontological sketch I have provided. In chapter 3, education is a way of being within Being. In chapter 4, study is a way of subsisting. And in chapter 5, the human person is a way of existing. In chapter 6, we look at them all together and consider their relative importance.

To understand the organization of the content of these chapters in relation and proportion to each of their organizing categories, consider the trinitarian lens with each chapter's theme taking the place of the ontological category (Being, subsistence, and existence) that it corresponds to:

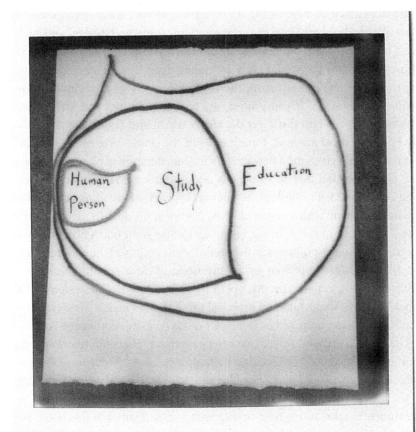

education, study, and the human person

While the content of these chapters does not orbit a bibliographic or scholarly concern—this is not intellectual history or a literature review—I cannot overstate the great impact that William James has had upon the entire work. Most significant for this study is James's pluralistic method. This is a hallmark of James's style: balance. His ideas ebb and flow as he adjusts his mind to the thing at hand and he has very little problem reversing order and taking up the thing he seemed to have jettisoned earlier. He expresses this well in his *Varieties* where he writes, "To understand a thing rightly we need to see it both out of its environment and in it, and to have acquaintance with the whole range of its variations."[37] This is consistent with his earlier psychological investigations that range from physiological descriptions to metaphysical and religious exhortations. James's methodological sensibility also bespeaks a deep understanding of human belief. The ultimate jury for his arguments is the stark reality of human experience. Rather than force himself into one's mind using the brute force of logical argumentation, James simply says: "If you protest, my friend, wait until you arrive there yourself!"[38] This pluralistic yet decidedly realist and realistic approach to the philosophical method, combined with the gentle force of his religious sensitivity, has given me a new vision for a folk iteration of phenomenology.

I understand that, to some, it is odd to think of William James as being concerned with ontology or phenomenology. Many think of James in shared company with someone like A. J. Ayer in his disdain for metaphysics.[39] Make no mistake: this popular caricature is an outrightly mistaken reading of James's philosophical system.[40] Perhaps it is a failure to read him at all. This is easily proven by an afternoon of close reading. One could choose James's *Pragmatism* that opens by affirming G. K. Chesterton's claim that "the most important and practical thing about a man is his view of the universe";[41] selections of his *Principles of Psychology*; portions of *Varieties of Religious Experience*; all of that brief gem that is *Human Immortality*; his unfinished textbook for teaching metaphysics, *Some Problems of Philosophy*; or any significant portions of his extensive letters and correspondence.

Interpretive controversy aside, there is more than exegetic fidelity or sentimental value to my relationship with William James in this book. He, along with the steadfast help of many dear friends and mentors, has challenged me in many of his texts—most recently in his letters and correspondence—to allow myself to imagine the world with or without a book in hand, using the resources I have in front, around, and inside of me, without too much concern for a "system." It is his unique, yet never singular, companionship that gives me any reply whatsoever to the questions hidden in

---

37. James, *Varieties*, 23.

38. Ibid., 160.

39. This was the impression I had before seeing James in primary text and reading the account given by Fredrick Copleston, S.J., in his *History of Philosophy* (vol. 8, pt. 2).

40. The two foremost authorities on James of the previous century, his esteemed student Ralph Barton Perry and John D. McDermott, both support this point in their life-long work on James. More recently, Robert Richardson's erudite biography—*William James: In the Maelstrom of American Modernism*—is also faithful to these readings of James.

41. James, *Pragmatism*, 1.

the lessons of my son Tomas, Heidegger, Warnick, and many others I am remiss to leave unmentioned.

Now, it seems appropriate to begin the work at hand with this artistic exhortation from William James, that reminds us that metaphysics as art can constitute a folkloric reversal: "There must in short be metaphysicians. Let us for a while become metaphysicians ourselves."[42]

42. James, *Problems of Philosophy*, 34.

Three

The Mystery of Education

Not only that *anything* should be, but that this very thing should be, is mysterious!

It is not probable that the reader will be satisfied with any of these solutions, and contemporary philosophers, even rationalistic ones, have on the whole agreed that no one has intelligibly banished the mystery of *fact*.

WILLIAM JAMES, *SOME PROBLEMS OF PHILOSOPHY*

INTRODUCTION

What is education? This question takes the very thing that education might be as the thing for investigation. In this chapter, I will discuss the complexities and distinctions embedded in this question and other questions like it. Ontological questions: questions about being (as opposed to meaning). Some will be particular issues within the philosophy of education, and others will be more general philosophical issues, yet neither should be excluded from the other.

A query of a thing within Being is one thing, but trying to account for a thing's context, for the thing within which a thing is, can be very easily taken for granted. A pure analysis of Being itself is impossible, yet even to account for things that stand in as contextual ontologies is difficult. Questions within the category of Being sit at a peculiar distance, ever-present yet never quite in full view. It is no surprise then, that ontological analysis of this kind is scarce within the field of Education,[1] or anywhere. The questions of Being are the most difficult questions imaginable, because they are not easy to imagine without being taken for granted. To ask such questions with regard to education, then, will also prove to be difficult. The difficulty lies in the fundamentality of Being and, I will claim, education. It is so fundamental that it is easily forgotten or ignored.

Imagine trying to spend a week fully aware of every breath taken. It would be impossible. Breathing is so fundamental that it is easily ignored and forgotten. It is taken for granted, but it is undeniably fundamental and serious and cannot stop. We all know we should not arbitrarily unplug a respirator. The same is true for this analysis, and any ontological analysis of Being. The rigor requires paying attention to something that has become habitually ignorable, something fundamental that sits outside of our senses. We seek Being because it is not yet observable to us, because it escapes our gaze, hidden in plain view. It is sought after not because it is rare, but because it is ubiquitous and ever-present. Constant. Concealed in the excess of its disclosure.

Heidegger was keenly aware that ontological research often loses sight of Being. He writes,

> Basically, all ontology, no matter how rich and firmly compacted a series of categories it has at its disposal, remains blind and perverted from its ownmost aim, if it has not first adequately clarified the meaning of Being, and conceived this clarification as its fundamental task.[2]

If this is true, then Heidegger's now famous claim that the question of Being had been forgotten, made when he drafted *Being and Time* in the 1920s, continues to be true almost one hundred years later, especially within the academic and professional field of Education.

Heidegger is not alone in this attitude about the fundamentality of Being. James makes similar claims in *Some Problems of Philosophy*, such as this one: "The question of being is the darkest in all philosophy."[3] And, within this darkness, James maintains, "Philosophy, in order not to lose

---

1. I will continue to use the capitalized version of this word to distinguish the ideological, professionalized, and schooled notion of *Education* from the simple and fundamental sort of *education* that I am interested in.

2. Heidegger, *Being and Time*, 31.

3. James, *Problems of Philosophy*, 46.

human respect, must take some notice of the actual constitutions of reality."[4] Philosophy of education is needed in Education because it can perform an ontological analysis that addresses the fundamentality of Being and the "actual constitutions of reality" with respect to its *raison d'être*, and namesake, education. The ontological questions that have not been sustained fully are questions of what education is, might be, and become. Education nowadays is assumed to be the case.

While there is much knowledge *about* education, we know very little of it: too much knowing-about, too little knowing. For instance, educational theories usually take "education" to be the case, in a very particular way, in advance. "Education" is usually assumed to be a thing in the first place. Where are the theories that bring the thing of education into question? Where can we find descriptive relief to precede theoretical and epistemological knowledge-about the thing? Even now, despite all caution to the contrary, education is simply assumed to be a thing, and it remains a presupposed fact unto itself, an inbred *primum mobile*, a credulous *causa sui*, a naïve assumption supported by the basic fact that to consider something is to consider it "as if" it were something. The questions that follow this presumption, if it is allowed to carry on without resistance, can only be pseudo-questions.

It is commonplace to find these pseudo-questions, and worse, within the academic literature of the field called "Education." James once wrote these candid words on his distaste for what he called "pedagogic literature" in a letter to G. Stanley Hall: "Pedagogic literature seems to contain such vast quantities of chaff that one hardly knows where to seek for the grain."[5] This "grain" James speaks of is the core, the essential content which is always sought: we seek the pregnant seed of eros, our desire to be within, to be with, to dwell within Being. With regard to "pedagogic literature," James did not live to read many of the educational writings written by the man he often referred to in print as "Professor Dewey," who remains the most influential philosopher of education in the English-speaking world today.

John Dewey shows a great deal of sensitivity to the fundamental questions of education, especially in the opening chapters of *Democracy and Education*. Years later, in *Experience and Education*, he makes this even clearer in his recommendation for how to think about "educational problems." He

4. James, *Problems of Philosophy*, 15.

5. William James, *William James: Selected Unpublished Correspondence, 1885—1910*, ed. Frederick J. Down Scott (Columbus, OH: Ohio State University Press, 1986), 34.

writes, "It is often well in considering educational problems to get a start by temporarily ignoring the school and thinking of other human situations."[6] For Dewey, as for James, education is not something fixed to a small and temporary institutional subject-matter. For Dewey, education takes us out into the waters of social life and culture. Yet, although Dewey ambitiously describes the political anatomy of education, he does not treat it as an ontological context. In fact, Dewey seems to oppose the idea that education could function as such a thing, placing it within experience and the formation of culture. Therefore, unlike Dewey, I hope to describe education as a context in the widest and most literal sense, using the phenomenological approach outlined in the previous chapter.

As Heidegger noted previously, phenomenologists are not immune to missing the ontological question. For instance, the Husserlian phenomenologist J. Gordon Chamberlin only grazes—and ultimately misses—the point in "Phenomenological Methodology and Understanding Education," a chapter in the collection of essays published in 1974 as *Existentialism and Phenomenology in Education*. There, he writes:

> Traditionally educators have assumed that one first works out or adopts a philosophical position and then proceeds to discern its implications for education. A phenomenological approach challenges that deductive procedure. Its method draws educators to look first at the thing itself in careful reflection on the meaning of education, for until it is clear what education is it will be unclear how philosophy and education are, or may be, related.[7]

In this passage, Chamberlin rightly makes the methodological imperative of phenomenology—"To the things themselves!"—clear. He seems to be concerned with what education is, with the object that it is. Nonetheless, his approach is hermeneutic, not ontological; it is interpretive, not descriptive. He is concerned with "careful reflection on the meaning of education." This concern is not the same thing as a careful reflection on the *being* of education. Because of this, Chamberlin is ultimately unable to answer to the call of phenomenology to return to phenomena, to things.[8]

6. As we have seen, following Heidegger, I find the treatment of education as a "problem" to be ironically problematic.

7. J. Gordon Chamberlin, "Phenomenological Methodology and Understanding Education," in *Existentialism and Phenomenology in Education*, ed. David E. Denton (New York: Teachers College Press, 1974), 119.

8. For Heidegger, the philosophical task takes up the "meaning of Being" through fundamental ontology, whereas—as Jean-Luc Marion argues in *God Without*

Even Heidegger concerns himself primarily with the *meaning* of Being in relation to time, not with the *being* of Being in relation to itself—even as he clarifies the project of fundamental ontology. Indeed the only ontologically grounded book to appear on the phenomenology of education is Eduardo Duarte's *Being and Learning*, where he offers an ontological exercise of self-disclosure that anchors Being to natality, forming the ontogenetic idea of "ceaseless nativity."[9] Duarte's ontological project is the clear exception, however, and this book seeks to build on that ontological and poetic project into the folk phenomenology we find in the relations between Being, subsistence, and existence. Nonetheless, Duarte awakens philosophy of education to its radical call to be foundational and this reminds us, again, of the great forgetting of Being.

This radical forgetting of Being in philosophy and education cannot be because of any technical problems or deficiencies. Despite varying amounts of capacities and interests, we all seem to inevitably run the marathon starting at different points in the race, with little to no regard for its starting line. We find ourselves in mid-flight, *in media res*, with no idea of where we came from. If we deny this, we are indicted by our own denial. The point here, then, is not to accomplish the analysis of the being of Being, the being of education, or the limited but real sense in which education is best understood as a descriptive analog to Being. Instead, it is to begin and end with the first question and, from that point, order all other questions accordingly. Otherwise, our visions of reality are at risk of ontological disorder, inversion, and subsequent infidelity to reality.

Whatever education might be is certainly out of order in its everyday linguistic usage. It is alarming that it has become conventional in contemporary society—and even within the academic field called Education—to think of education as completely indistinguishable from, and in some cases synonymous with, the compulsory schooling system recently instituted under the authority of the similarly recent political apparatus of the day, the nation-state. It has become ordinary language to substitute the terms "education" and "schooling" freely and carelessly. Sometimes my students ask about the *educational* merits of things that seem to be unrelated to the literal and narrow time and space of a modern school's classroom. Many

---

Being—theology moves past Being as a thing for interpretation and begins to reduction of givenness through the disclosure of revelation.

9. Eduardo M. Duarte, *Being and Learning: A Poetic Phenomenology of Education*, (Rotterdam: 2012).

others share this view, too. While the earlier theories I mentioned have serious contributions to make, this narrow view is utterly ahistorical and absurd. It errs in thinking of education as the exclusive subject matter of the schools and states of the recent past. A similar view of politics, for example, would be dismissed outright as a sophomoric genealogy, and for good reason.[10] This terminological issue is a serious category mistake, even within philosophy of education. How odd is it that a field of scholars so frequently invokes terms that have no consistency or clarity regarding their meaning and descriptive reference?

Scanning the spectrum of educational thought, this much seems clear: *Educational theories have never accounted for the being of education, for what education is, and much less for education as a context for study and the human person.*[11] This is not to say that the question has not been asked at all, but to suggest instead that it has not been asked in a way that believed itself and took action accordingly. At best, we have epistemological or political theories *about* education, symptomatic meanderings that cannot fundamentally address its ontological is-ness, its reality as thing, its being-within Being. These are theories in which education is presumed to be a thing in advance and only related to this or that other thing *afterwards*, in an order that proceeds from Being but pays it no—or only very little—attention. How can we understand education if we have never tried, failed, and tried again to know it?

I suspect that during this study I will find myself in the same position attempting to imagine what education might be, as when I face that haunting question "Who am I?" with any ontological seriousness or insight. And, perhaps, I may come to realize that these two questions, "What is education?" and "Who am I?" are not entirely different or unrelated to each other. Both will require a reply that says the least amount possible, since the subject matter verges on ineffability.

---

10. As an example, imagine the sheer ignorance of a political theory that took politics to be the exclusive product of modern politics, the progeny of the upheavals of Tudor England in the 16th century or, to be more generous, the unification of Spain a century earlier. How, then, could such an impoverished genealogy hold any mettle for education?

11. One can test this claim very easily by asking people—from whom one cares to hear an opinion—what they think education is. The results will surely fail to disprove my thesis. And I do not intend to extend it any further in this study.

FEARFUL OBJECTIONS

Although there are fierce, interesting, and well-known critics of metaphysics and ontology within the academic discipline of philosophy, I have more often been told that these kinds of questions are pointless or dangerous to ask in the disciplinary field called Education. I have been asked things like the following: Who cares about Being (or being) in Education? That's not what Education is about. How will you raise graduation rates and test scores by asking these kinds of questions? What about the dropouts and teacher burn out? What difference will it make in the real world? What are the policies you will write or analyze with this?

Beyond the initial delight I take to these objections, since they are fraught with ontological implications, I wonder about the content of the questions themselves. It is almost as though there is a traumatic risk lying in the recognition of ontological analysis as a valid, and therefore dangerous, form of inquiry. Given the lack of answers I have offered thus far, strong objections would seem a bit premature, but it is not entirely unwarranted.

I know (*conocer*) that my own aversion to asking myself the same sorts of questions—curiosities about my own being within Being, my own place in the world—is because I am afraid. I fear the answers, or even worse, the lack thereof. I fear the unknown, the unconscious, and the possibility of nothing in the place where I desire to find something. I fear not being, or being alone. Alienation. More often than not, I do not wish to have the thing that my self is (whatever that could be) rendered suspect and brought into question.

Perhaps it is the same way for the study of education: Could it be this very thing—fear—that motivates educational aversions to ontological investigation? It doesn't seem out of the question. After all, these examinations could lead us to believe that education is very different than we once thought it was. Or even more radically, that it is nothing at all. So why gamble with the potential of losing that pleasant fantasy of education-as-we-knew-it? Especially when to many of us in and out of the field, "education" has become something like an appendage of who we think ourselves to be. Furthermore, acknowledged realities demand a certain degree of action. What if education reveals itself as something that makes demands on our ways of living that we would rather not meet? What if we are forced to change?

And then there is the integrity of our ego: What if these ontological questions hurt our feelings? According to the contemporary Freudian psychoanalyst, Deborah Britzman, questions like these *will* hurt our feelings. On a panel entitled "Convergences and Trajectories in Curriculum Theory," at the 2009 Bergamo Conference for Curriculum Theorizing, she began her commentary by making this simple, yet profound, point regarding psychoanalysis: "The reason so many people oppose psychoanalysis in education is because it hurts their feelings." Knowing very little about psychoanalysis myself, I am not sure if this is true, although I intuitively suspect that it is. True or not, it does seem like it could be the case in much of the educational aversion to ontology, phenomenology, and philosophy.

Ontological questions are met with suspicion, at least in part, because of the same desire that makes them in the first place. After all, what is held suspect could not possibly be ontology outright. Who can question being within Being? What could be an alternative to it that is not nihilism? What is considered suspicious could only be the reality that ontological research threatens the current embedded ontological assumptions, the "facts" of the day. Those sacred facts may or may not be explicitly acknowledged, but they certainly are the case by their sheer presumed *facticity* (a pejorative term for Heidegger). Otherwise, where else could these objections come from? It is my view that most of us do not want to discover that the realities our lives are built upon might merely be facts and nothing else. What if things are not as we once thought—and perhaps even believed!—that they were, even if the discovery is mysterious, uncertain, excessive, and incomplete, or precisely *because* the discovery might be mysterious! In spite of these understandably fearful objections, reality compels us to account for it.

Keep in mind the previous chapter and where this ontological curiosity began: in the everyday objections of a three-year-old. Because of this ordinary and worldly origin, I hope that you will see that the simplicity of the question "What is education?" does not merely feign at acting simple and should also reveal itself to be extremely practical. As I said earlier: reality demands action. How else, then, can we act by doing things we assume to be the case unless we have some clue as to what is the case to begin with? We cannot superstitiously presume things to be things and then believe that taking these fantasies hook, line, and sinker through unquestioned "action" is a way of acting in the world—or of acting at all. This is why theory and practice cannot work in a vacuum or a linear progression, at least not before we give the facts of the day some critical contemplation, again and again. This is the skeptical core of what we might call, following Foucault and Nietzsche and recognizing as beginning with Descartes, a "critical ontology": the continuous study of things in the world we presume to be the case to see if they *are* what we take them to *be*. A phenomenological reduction tests whether the thing is what we were told it was or if it is something else—or even whether it is nothing at all. Even if the meaning of the thing escapes in the end. Even if all we are left with is a meaningless thing that *is* nonetheless itching away at our deepest, most unconscious desires and curiosities.

My purpose, in this chapter dedicated to the lens of Being in relation to education is not to unveil that mysterious fog from the reality of what education might be. It is actually the reverse. The purpose of this study is to advocate for re-enchantment: *to re-enchant education with mystery*. By simply raising the ontological question, we begin to see that things are all mysterious to the core. All I can possibly hope for is that education emerges as just such a thing, dark and mysterious. I hope that education will be recognized as a mystery and that we will be moved to face it within that dark reality: the paradox of its apophatic ontology. Can we remove our sandals, tremble, and wonder as we stare into its curiously burning and dancing flames, unable to forget it when we go to sleep, walk along the sidewalk, or step into (or out of) a classroom? This would begin to propose a strong alternative to the deeply disenchanted notions of education that take no interest whatsoever in education as a thing and desperately invent preposterous epistemological certainties and psychometrics for account-able learning, and responsible jobs for the living dead. This would begin to recover a sense of what is at stake in the school that we hope to be the prog-eny of this thing that might become education: The being and becoming of human persons, those endangered subjects of modern schools and society.

HOPE AND NOVELTY[12]

Hope, as I imagine her to be—indeed, as I *hope* for her to be—is neither an optimist nor a pessimist. Her proverbial cup is only what it is. She is an ongoing, insatiable desire for something real and true. At the very least, she is the desire for something that matters to my widest self and the world I inhabit. She is a desire for something that is at once old and new, like real pleasure or true love. Hope appears as desire and the intuition that this longing might actualize in beauty, that there is something beauti-ful in the world—that the world itself might be beautiful. Growing tired or bored seems to describe the times when I lose hope and begin to feel

12. For more on the issue of novelty read the final five chapters of James's *Some Problems of Philosophy* with special attention to chapters nine and ten, "The Problem of Novelty" and "Novelty and the Infinite," respectively.

presumptuous and arrogant or despondent and despairing, when I begin to think of the world as disproportionate and unfaithful to itself. I suspect that this is more than a private eccentricity. I am even led to believe that this may even be true for many other people.

I bring this up subject because the objections to ontology mentioned in the previous section are also well-known objections to philosophy in general. They often appear in two forms. In the first, they say something like this: *Philosophy is perennially hopeless.* It duplicates itself over and over like a senile, skipping record that repeats the childish question "Why?" with no regard for who is listening. There is no hope that it will end or comfort us with anything but more nagging questions that fester like a shallow splinter in the tender flesh of the palm, questions of life and death and immortality. Facing this perennial hopelessness, philosophy appears to be irrelevant, otherworldly, self-absorbed, and senselessly painful.

And then there is the second accusation: *Philosophy is hopelessly perennial.* Everything there is to think has been thought. Everything there is to write has been written. Facing this hopeless perennialism, the very thought of self-expression seems futile since there is nothing new to say and, perhaps, nothing new to be. At best, there is study. But, as we will see in the next chapter, study can often seem barren for the exact same reasons.[13]

But all is not lost. In spite of these charges against philosophy, things catch our attention and *philo-sophia* (love of wisdom) emerges. Wonder embeds itself in the wonderful, curiosity is infectious once we find something to arouse our curiosity, and awe is hidden within the beautiful—even the beautifully ugly. We desire Desire. The trick seems to be in finding something *desirable*, something attention-worthy and worthwhile. This is what philosophy, ontology, and phenomenological methods are to and for me: They are an offering of something desirable, attention-worthy, and worthwhile to do and be. They offer the art of study as an inescapable way of subsistence. In and through these studies I am led to believe that there is reason to be hopeful for something new out there, that there is ever-ancient and ever-new beauty to find, become, and be-with and within. For me, this hope was rekindled in a special way during my study of the work of Jean-Luc Marion, who personally sent me to re-read Heidegger and Nietzsche. There I found similarities that paralleled my study of the works of William James—all of them surrounding the question of Being. What is this hope I found in these bookish studies? The hope that philosophy is not over and has only just begun.

13. Maybe this is why so many students hate school and so many people seem to hate education and their life in general?

In the philosophical quandary of Being we find at the turn of the 20th century—the predicament that finally seemed poised to replace the medieval study of God's existence—we recognize an entirely new and excessive world to be discovered and awed by, not unlike Albert Einstein's magnificent correction and expansion of Isaac Newton's universe. Contemporary to Einstein's revolution in physics, we find a rigorous philosophical examination of Being as a thing for investigation in a way that neither abandoned the *philosophia perennis* nor remained completely faithful to it. It continued the work of the Enlightenment and rejected modernity all at once.

This was not only a secluded affair of academics and scholars. It literally created and shaped, and has been constituted and formed in turn, by the times (*Geist*). Who can imagine Red October without the precedent of *Capital* and *The Communist Manifesto*; *Being and Nothingness* and *Nausea* without the precedent of World War II; or May '68 without all of the above? This is exciting! It is also tragic. Besides the euphoria and sobriety that it brings, it is also a reason—perhaps *the* reason—to speak of ontological research, phenomenology, and philosophy with any glimmer of hope that it can and perhaps will yield anything desirable, attention-worthy, and worthwhile to the thing we call "education."

Here we find a preliminary sense of education. Education seems to be the very hope I have described. We hope for education to be the case not because we know it, but because we desire for whatever it might be to be something that has the potency and capacity for beauty, excitement, novelty, and tragedy. Education as hope is the preparation for the mystery of education, and for education as mystery.

REAL, TRUE MYSTERY

One of the perplexing curiosities of Being is that it often resembles a never-ending Russian doll or an eternal onion. It is layered like numbers (mathematics), matter (physics), and the cosmos (astronomy). As a whole, it is bigger than our ability to imagine it, and its parts are equally as small. Being's only invitation seems to be into infinity. It comes in no other size but excess and demands nothing less than humility and restlessness.[14]

---

14. Sigmund Freud describes this disturbing experience as the religiously relevant "oceanic feeling" in the opening to *Civilization and Its Discontents* (London: Hogarth Press, 1930). To be fair, he also claims that he has never experienced it himself.

How, then, does one attempt to examine such a thing? An inquiry into Being is not unlike the work of a detective. In a mystery novel, detective work surprises our intuitions and disturbs our beliefs and investments in the story. We often find that the most likable and least objectionable character turns out to be the villain. The work of the detective is embedded in her namesake: to *detect* what is the case in a situation that appears mysterious. And the image of a quintessential detective carries a lens to see things through. Let us think of ourselves the same way: as detectives holding a trinitarian lens in our hand to seek, sense, and see things with.

This is what names and classifies the genre of literature we find detectives in: mystery novels. From Sherlock Holmes to Scooby-Doo, detective work is especially good at taking supernatural tricks and revealing their natural operations, coincidences, or conspiracies. A detective always works with the conviction that there is something going on. A detective never works in the midst of nothing. In other words, what is of utmost importance in this genre of literature and research is that something must be the case to begin with. A mystery cannot exist in the midst of nothing. Mystery cannot be nothing; it cannot be an absent void. It may lack meaning, but it cannot be outside of Being.

Even though Being is such a profound mystery, escaping the grasp of every attempt to capture it, it is not supernatural. It is not of another world. That is the point of Heidegger's notion of Being-in-the-world: Being is never ahistorical, it is the very condition upon which history becomes possible. This worldly notion of Being does not make it any less mysterious. It does insist that the mystery of Being cannot be an absence that is ontologically negative. It must be. It must be something instead of nothing. And to be, it must be in-the-world. Mystery is not like the "evil" we find in privation theory, where "evil" has no Being of its own without acting as a parasite on something that is. Unlike this view of evil, mystery is not a parasitic reality. It is not the negation of the real, or the negative side of the truth. Mystery is a positive absence. Absence *within* Being: an absence of disclosure, knowledge, or meaning is not the absence of Being itself. Mystery is very dark to our sight, to be sure, but it is neither the unknown that is nothing at all nor the impossible that is never actually possible or possibly actual. Quite the reverse: mystery, like everything else, is something.

For this reason, mystery is a profound truth and an imposing reality. This truth and reality is unknown because of its excess, *not* because of its lack. It is always too much, never too little. The excess of mystery saturates our ability to see it and convert what it is into meaning. It does not destroy itself because it cannot be seen or grasped and made into meaning. Because we can never see a mystery in proportion to its wholeness, it is also impossible in a radical sense. It saturates possibility.

That the world is mysterious is itself a truth and a reality. It may tell us nothing, but that is not to be confused with being no-thing. Its meaninglessness does not annihilate its Being. Mystery is the least and the most we can say, all at once, with any amount of positive certainty. We can be certain that there has been, is, and will be mystery.

Even to deny this would itself be very mysterious and demand an explanation that is unknowable to the believer and impossible to speak or symbolize. It would be like someone declaring a riveting mystery novel to be certain and boring. Or, if the novel had its final three chapters missing—like Dickens's *Mystery of Edwin Drood*, which was never finished—it would be like someone who had read it with great interest later declaring to have no desire whatsoever to know what the ending might have been. In a more serious way, it would be like an orphan who never wondered about her biological and genealogical origins, or a person who has never felt something strange and wondered about it. Given the mystery that we find education to be, it would be like an educator who never wondered what education really and truly is—or who forgot about the ontological wonder within this question altogether.

To a skeptic, so many declarations and assertions about the reality and truth of mystery might verge on the paradoxical. This would not be unjustified. Skeptical or not, you too might wonder: "If the unknown is real, then, how do we really know this reality?" These are surely word games that might be instructive, but they are not intended to prove or disprove the stated thesis of the positive ontology—and negative epistemology—of mystery any more than the thesis itself. Mystery is what the artist knows when she does not know what to do, when the performance and craft is the only content.

To someone predisposed to believe such a thing, my claims will probably seem believable. To another who is predisposed not to believe these things, my claims will seem circular, tautological, and perhaps useless. As James put it, "If you have a God already whom you believe in, these arguments confirm you. If you are an atheist, they fail to set you right."[15] And to someone whose feelings have not yet made up her mind in advance,

---

15. James, *Varieties*, 428.

one feeling will likely prevail, demand that she look elsewhere for further confirmation, or disinterest might take the day and she might forget the whole thing entirely. Even this range of options is itself quite perplexing, giving way to mysteries of its own.

RELIGION VS. IDEOLOGY

This probable set of predictions (noted above) is one reason why everyone is unavoidably religious: we all hold fast to any number of beliefs or creeds. This sense of religiosity begins to point us in the right direction. Anyone who thoroughly hates religion does so religiously. And yet, no one goes through life without a creed of some kind. Religious belief is not without its uncertainties. Religious convictions are steeped in uncertainty that gives way to mystery, to the unknown.

Consider behaviorism, atheism, and theism. What these creeds cannot deny is that there are things that give them fits. For behaviorists, the life of the mind and the experience of love and loving (among other things) constantly elude their grasp. For the atheist, the theistic possibility that there is a God is impossible to dispel with absolute certainty. For the theist, the atheistic possibility that there is no God—or that, if there is one, it is only a human invention—is a possibility that all too often seems to be true. Even in other things (hobbies, sports, politics, and other nostalgic affiliations) we find that everyone carries some form of devotion to any number of articles of faith that constitute their belief and their creed, and there are always ready counterfactuals.

If religious creed is taken to be this inescapable condition of belief, then its generic psychological dimension does not merit serious controversy. What is susceptible to the dangers of fundamentalism and superstition would not be religion or belief outright. Only when our beliefs become ideological would religion then become disturbing. This disturbance would not be for moral or ethical reasons. It would be for ontological reasons. Again, like a detective novel—where the problem is not the criminal or immoral nature of the "crime" but, instead, what is or is not the case—so too with ideology: basic psychological belief is a religious condition and expression that simply is the case. Ideology, however, distorts reality into something that is not the case. This distortion is deceptive and its dishonesty is not "immoral" so much as it is simply ontologically false, untrue, and unfaithful to reality.

What is striking about the difference between generic religious belief and fundamentalist ideology is the striking absence of a critical ontology and, consequently, the disenchanting castration of mystery from the life of the ideologue. Puritanical ecclesiologies, positivist scientism, and neo-liberal economic fantasies share this aspect of being thoroughly ideological. They display more than the simple psychological religiosity of human belief. They claim to have a rather comprehensive account of revelation. They may admit a finite number of mysteries that remain, but will maintain that what has been revealed is more valuable than what remains concealed; what has been disclosed is sufficient to merit devotion to their creed. They often bolster these accounts with terrifying—and terribly effective—eschatologies and soteriologies. Among them, we find an ideological account of Education.

Under ideological influence, Education can appear to be frightening and even apocalyptic. Anyone slightly familiar with the controversies of educational policy in federal and state schooling agendas knows that many people are very worried about things going badly for them if they neglect this magical thing called "Education." As early as the Common School Movement of the 1830s we find statesmen promoting compulsory schooling as a way to expand "educational opportunity," thereby preventing moral corruption and social degradation. Take these words from Horace Mann as an example:

> Let the common school be expanded to its capabilities, let it be worked to the efficiency of which it is susceptible, and nine-tenths of the crimes in the penal code would become obsolete; the long catalogue of human ills would be abridged; men would walk more safely by day; every pillow would be more inviolable by night; property, life, and character held by a stronger tenure; all rational hopes respecting the future brightened.[16]

The "educational" rhetoric of more recent times has not become any less alarmist. The 1983 report *Nation at Risk* uses bellicose rhetoric that compares the neglect of "Education" as an equivalent to committing a form of "disarmament." It even goes so far as to suggest that such a disarming force from another nation-state would be considered an "act of war." *No Child Left Behind* refers to the neglect of "Education" as the abandonment of children. This act's title brings to mind a popular apocalyptic Evangelical

---

16. Mann, *Life of Horace Mann*, vol. 1 (Boston: 1865), 142.

book series *Left Behind*.[17] There is an unmistakably apocalyptic tone to these warnings sold as reform, and for good reason: Education has become messianic. Under these accounts, Education has moved from generic religious belief to a fundamentalist ideology. Lacking ontological critique and investigation, it exists supernaturally as a form of magic or superstition. It fetishizes the power of "science-based research" and peddles these certainties with a powerful message of salvation. Education, under these terms, is the redeemer who saves children and the nation-state from neglect and damnation, from being "left behind" in the global economy.

The salvation narrative—we might call it "schoolvation"—goes something like this: If you go to school and act rightly, according to the selected teachings handed down by the Church and entrusted to the priests and priestesses, you will be one of the elect. The Educated. But not all at once. Your name will gradually be written on scrolls called "diplomas" and "credentials," signed by the high priests called "principals," "superintendents," "deans," and "presidents." With enough degrees of piety, you will eventually be saved from the damnation that is a life uneducated, unsaved by the school, unwritten in the transcripts of the Book of Life. "Stay in school" and you will not suffer the torment that comes with not getting this magical thing called an Education. Stay in school long enough and you will be entrusted with a respectable social status and responsible work. Then, you will be saved.

Those who have grown up in material poverty have likely heard this "Gospel of Schoolvation" preached to them by righteous men and women, and believed it. After all, who really wants to go to hell or, even worse, be poor? So, in fear of damnation, Education becomes that one thing that can get a full-ride scholarship, for some, or college admission, for others, leading to the promised land of milk and honey that lacks the curse of invisibility and shame brought by poverty. People proclaim their gospel: Education is the way, the truth, and the light. But, to many, it merely seems to be a reliable way out of the fear of being looked down upon and treated poorly, a way to learn self-hatred by slowly and meticulously gouging out those sensitive eyes, conveniently blinding oneself to those wretched, invisible poor people—including the proud parents. Education becomes something altogether unrelated to its noble titles and its mysterious reality: it becomes

17. See National Defense Education Act of 1958, 85th Cong., P.L. 85–864 (September 2, 1958); National Commission on Excellence in Education, *A Nation at Risk: The Imperative for Educational Reform* (Washington, DC: US Government Printing Office, 1983), http://www.ed.gov/pubs/NatAtRisk/index.html; and No Child Left Behind Act of 2001.

a way to survive the apocalypse of the present. And in the deepest and most truthful intuitions, it is clear that Education is purely instrumental and not to be believed in.

For the rich, I am told that this meta-narrative is just as ominous. I hear that for the wealthy, "schoolvation" is a way to retain proper social class and avoid disappointing already opulent parents, family, and friends who thoroughly expect the doctrine of "schoolvation" to preserve privilege, status, and success.

This messianic narrative and its articles of faith are not learned overnight. They require a great deal of catechesis in order to formalize the doctrines of the school as an "educational" site of exception and redemption. They require obedience. Obedience is best achieved by removing the mysterious and disenchanting the thing in question—or denying its very being, its thingness—so that it can be controlled and regulated by the superstitions of ideological certainty. Rejecting mystery and keeping detectives at bay secures a hegemonic monopoly over the reality of education and the school. With that monopoly comes a straightjacket of the imagination and reliance on a creed that is not religious. It is ideological.

The ecclesiology of Education, like all other churches, requires a superstitious sense of divinity to be taken seriously by a large number of people. Therefore, since Education seems to have already acquired the status of a god, asking questions about its being could help to find out whether this creed is truly under divine right or if it is simply a magic trick, a coincidence, or a conspiracy. Does this god exist? What is the nature of its being? Furthermore, it could illuminate whether the moralistic, bellicose, and morbid threats made by Whigs of the past and present are generic religious beliefs or dangerous ideologies.

It is my suspicion that superstitious and fundamentalist accounts of Education are a major reason why "educational" research is guarded from ontological investigation: it has established an unquestioned monopoly over the imaginary of its being. Education has no need to take an inward turn, we are told by its guardians. In response to these repressive conceptions of Education, a purely reactionary move would be misguided. This is not a reason to abandon or dismiss the school or the academic and professional fields altogether. The power that Education and the school yield is not only indicative of the power of false superstition; it is also an example of religious experience in general—even in the realm of the secular. For this very reason, we need something like another Reformation; something like a second Enlightenment; something that can only begin by bringing the most sacred thing, Education, into question through the rigor of reduction and study. This is the first reason why education is mysterious: everything begins within Being, within mystery, and remains so until it is revealed and disclosed, offered and shown.

In the section to follow, let us begin to look further at the constitution of education and schooling. Then, we will consider some other aspects of the mystery of education.

POLITICS AND PSYCHOLOGY

The politics of schooling are very easily confused with the psychological aspects of teaching, and in both cases a contextual ontology of education is missed. This is not to belittle one or the other, nor to try and say that they are mutually exclusive when seen in full view. Instead, it is to suggest that there are differences between the two that are more than trivial and to disaggregate some of the common sense notions by relying on the trinitarian lens. Here are two reasons: First, within the realm of schooling and the practice of teaching we can find different things going on. In schooling, we find political things happening: a *polis* (a state or a community), rhetoric (instruction), and constitution (policies and curricula aimed at the formation and preservation of the *polis*). In teaching, we find psychological things happening: thought and thinking, consciousness, the life of the mind, the eros of study (the subject of chapter 4), and the human person as teacher (the subject of chapter 5). Second, there is also a spatial component that distinguishes them. Schooling directly refers to the school. Schools are concrete, perceptual places and spaces. Teaching refers to a conceptual place within mind, consciousness, and the world at large that is not so easily placed. It is not as expansive as education, but it is more generalizable across a context of education than schooling. Of the two, teaching is more instructive to us in relation to education and therefore more fecund and potent for the imagination.

At the same time, it would be premature to undervalue the school. After all, it, too, is a site within the mysterious context of education. And there is much that we can learn from the research done with regard to schooling. Despite the richness of a notion of education within Being, schooling has received much closer and more attention. While the reality of education has gone untouched, the school has by comparison been thoroughly put to the test, again and again, especially during the previous two centuries, after the advent of compulsory schooling. If the same attention were devoted to what is often presumed to be the school's educational source, we might begin to imagine what ontological research in and of education would look like. It would ask many of the same critical questions that have already been asked of the school by the field of philosophy of education for over a century, questions like, What is it exactly? Where did it come from? Why should it be taken seriously? Should it be abolished or not? Is it dead or alive?

Nonetheless, the questions would also differ because the politics of schooling presumably sits on the psychological shoulders of teaching, which severely misses an ontological notion of education or misappropriates it into political or psychological theory. That is to say that while schooling provides a way to imagine what ontological research of education might be like, it also lacks the ability to say much more than that since it re-emerges as questionable when we analyze the reality of education.

I would also like to suggest that this difference between the politics of the school and the psychology of teaching points to a profound synergy between them to not only distinguish education, but also to place themselves within the mystery of education. Rather than posit the sole view that politics and psychology, schools and teaching, are somehow crass while education is mysteriously profound and pure, we might begin to see that these are not two worlds but one.

I am deeply troubled by the totalizing *nihil obstat* contemporary society has given the State apparatus to practice compulsion via modern compulsory schooling and, to a much greater extent, the limits of the educational imagination therein. I am also troubled at how this has given rise to a particularly secular psychological image of the teacher, ignoring the wisdom traditions of teaching that predate it. But this is not the sole, nor the best, possible sense of schooling or teaching. In the dual happenings of politics and psychology we find a basic fact of life: we cannot separate our communal and social life from our innermost thoughts, feelings, and desires. To try and pretend to have accomplished such a feat would be utterly nihilistic. Yet both politics and psychology happen within an even wider context of Being, where we find the ontological place of a far more ambitious and mysterious notion of education.

This fact is displayed in relation to schooling and teaching in James's *Talks to Teachers on Psychology*. Despite his tone that sometimes verges on condescension towards the teaching profession, James brings the politics of schooling *and* the psychology of education to bear on the art of teaching. It is in the final movement of these talks where he uncovers the mystery of education. He ends his *Talks to Teachers* with these stirring words that unify the political and the psychological in the loving practice of teaching, which indicates the need for a further category beyond them:

> I have now ended these talks. If to some of you the things I have said seem obvious or trivial, it is possible that they may appear less so when, in the course of a year or two, you find yourselves noticing and apperceiving events in the schoolroom a little differently, in consequence of some of the conceptions I have tried to make more clear. I cannot but think that to apperceive your pupil as a little sensitive, impulsive, and reactive organism, partly fated and partly free, will lead to a better intelligence of all his ways. Understand him, then, as such a subtle little piece of machinery. And if, in addition, you can also see him *sub specie boni*, and love him as well, you will be in the best possible position for becoming perfect teachers.[18]

This passage is profound and challenging for many reasons. One of them is that, unlike the predominant view on schooling today, James's disposition to the school is remarkably optimistic. This optimism is somewhat bizarre for the tormented James who wrote on the absurdity of academic degrees in his witty essay "The Ph.D. Octopus."[19] Throughout his life he remained critical of formal structures that seemed to demand more respect than they were worth. Yet here he speaks of schooling with great warmth and hope. Given his record for skeptical dispositions toward institutions, where does James's peculiar optimism for the American school come from? The answer might be this: Throughout his *Talks to Teachers*, James's optimism flowed from his hope for what the school could be if its teachers would take the time and effort to know their students by learning about their psychological make-up in order to love them properly—to know-about them in order to know them. But James does not ultimately credit the political institution of schooling nor his psychological description of teaching—he points beyond, towards love.

Hardly one for naïve optimism, James's hope was not the product of superstition. He knew firsthand the profound effect that descriptive

---

18. James, *Talks to Teachers*, 196.

19. Besides critiquing the requisites of the PhD—a degree that he lacked, as his only degree was in medicine—James also did not support the founding of the American Philosophical Association, of which he later became president. See James, *Letters*.

psychological insight could have on the capacity for love, for understanding the community at large *and* the inner-workings of those mysteries we call "mind," "consciousness," and "self." He also included and celebrated philosophy and religious experience within this realm of life. Yet, like Dewey, James never offers an ontological description of education. It wasn't until his final posthumous text where we find him thinking about the problem of Being. There is indication of this elsewhere, but it is more indirect. For instance, he could not separate the life of the mind from the lives and minds of others in the condition he called "a certain blindness in human beings." This already reveals more than a psychological gap in understanding, something closer to an ontological condition. This is further supported by his sense of a "pluralistic universe," where in place of dogmatic dualisms he posited "the flux." In phenomenological fashion, James argued that we must turn *towards* this flux of life, not away from it.[20] He writes, "Dive back into the flux [and] turn your face toward sensation, that fleshbound thing which rationalism has always loaded with abuse."

I find his complex, flux-facing view of politics and psychology deeply instructive to the task of phenomenology, while ultimately incapable of articulating an *ontological* description of education. And perhaps this is the point. Regardless, it is crucial to how one might continue to think of the looming ontological question ("What is education?") without turning to rash judgments or oversimplifications, and confusing the mystery of education with the politics of schooling or the psychology of teaching (and, as we will see, study). More than that, it reminds us that the world is complicated and mysterious and the contents therein follow suit by ontological necessity—and we are called to ontological fidelity.

THE DIVINE IS SERIOUS

In case this ontic quest is misunderstood, please take note that the question "What is education?" does not imply a hope for a singular thing to be found or a prescriptive principle to be obeyed. It is not my purpose here to stake a claim to the one true "being" of education and defend it against all comers. The aim is not to "define" education. We must describe, not define. I take Nietzsche's warning to heart that "only that which is without history can be defined."[21] Lacking a definition does not mean that there is nothing going on

20. James, *Writings*, 951 (enclosure mine).

21. Friedrich Nietzsche, *Genealogy of Morals*. In Max Scheler's treatment of

here. It simply means that, as James put it, "Philosophy lives in words, but truth and fact well up into our lives in ways that exceed verbal formulation. There is in the living act of perception always something that glimmers and twinkles and will not be caught . . ."[22] Let's see what we can glimpse!

Since education is assumed to be so many different things to so many different people, a sensible way to begin to look for its description would be with a claim like this: *Education is what it is to those who take it to be the case.* The question now becomes whether a cacophony of voices can be reduced into a more articulate expression of itself, beyond common sense or ordinary language. This is not to try to take the plural and make it one thing, but, instead, to ask: What, if anything, could we imagine such a plural thing to have in common? What makes this name *be* in these various ways without becoming utterly unspeakable and unknowable to those who speak it? What do those who speak about education as though they know it seem to imply that it is? Or, do they only know-about it? This much is clear: *Education remains a mystery to us.* Knowing-about education is not the same as knowing it. At this present moment, no one seems to know what education is.

A preliminary phenomenon we can filter out of these voices is that education is taken to be divine. This does not mean that people are acting ideologically about its divinity. It does mean that people are religious about it; they believe in it. What I mean is that people who take education to be the case, even those who deny it seem to take it to be something divine, in the sense of something that is serious. We can look to James's *Varieties* and see that education can be found in the divine phenomenon from which James comes to understand a minimalist "primal reality" of religion. This observation for James, and for myself, is not a definition of the divine; it is simply a sketch of a glimpse of reality. James writes, "The divine shall mean for us only such a primal reality as the individual feels impelled to respond to solemnly and gravely, and neither by curse nor jest."[23]

Ressentiment he presents this alternative to definition: "Instead of defining the word, let us briefly characterize or describe the phenomenon."

22. James, *Varieties*, 446–47.

23. A page earlier, James makes a similar remark concerning religion that embellishes these words: "There must be something solemn, serious, and tender about any attitude which we denominate religious. If glad, it must not grin or snicker; if sad, it must not scream or curse. It is precisely as being *solemn* experiences that I wish to interest you in religious experiences." James, *Varieties*, 39.

Now, isn't this exactly the same way we feel about education? That it is something solemn and of grave importance, something we cannot discard or take lightly? If someone were to talk about education as though it were trivial and unimportant, would we not rightfully object? And wouldn't this objectionable person rightly know—and perhaps be delighted—that they were committing a sort of blasphemy? We might even tell this heretic: "That is not education!"[24] We might ask them to recant or submit to further catechesis.

It seems safe to assume that we can find a common phenomenology in the discourse on education as something that, at the very least, is mysterious as a matter of practical difficulty to agree upon and, as such, is not a joking matter and should be taken very seriously. This is the first thing we can say about the mystery of education: it is serious in a way not unlike what anyone takes to be divine in its "primal reality." This divine sensibility is not an exclusive one. We might even call it panentheistic. In other words, the divinity of education is not superstitiously reserved away from the world. For this reason, the seriousness we find in attitudes about divinity and education are a sober mark of tragedy. This divine mark is especially visible when we face the dark invisibility of Being.

To develop sight for this, we must acquire tragic eyes. The trinitarian lens is a dark lens. These eyes are the mark of true philosophical wonder. As James put it, "The philosophic wonder thus becomes a sad astonishment, and like the overture to *Don Giovanni*, philosophy begins with a minor chord."[25] The cosmos sings the blues. This song tells us that it knows what love is, even if it has little to no knowledge-about it.[26]

TRAGEDY

In his *Poetics*, Aristotle declares tragedy to be an imitation of an action that is three things: serious, complete, and possessing magnitude.[27] If education is indeed serious like James's notion of the divine, then Aristotelian tragedy may serve to give a further sense of what education is, if the other two

---

24. This sentiment might explain why the use of state compulsion to enforce compulsory schooling laws is met with so little resistance over time: People seem to recognize the lurking divinity of education, its solemnity and its gravity.

25. James, *Some Problems*, 39.

26. This refers to the jazz standard "You Don't Know What Love Is," that teaches that until we know the Blues, we cannot know love—suffering begets love.

27. Aristotle, *Poetics*, trans. Hutton, 50.

categories (complete and possessing magnitude) are equally as descriptive as the first one (serious). In case this moves along uncritically, let us first consider one objection to the idea that education is serious.

I could imagine a critique that might claim that seriousness can go too far. This objector might say, "Count me out! I do not find education to be serious as you say it is. Can't we become too serious? Where is the room for levity?" From her view, education could also be taken *too* seriously. This critic might come from many points of view, she may even be a teacher who advocates for play and free time as ways to remove the "seriousness" of an overly restricting classroom and curricula. I do not necessarily disagree with her intent or her teaching methods, but I do think that this construal of what is meant by "serious" is a misunderstanding of what I am describing here.

To explain what I mean, imagine this scenario: While my sons and I are out for a walk, the younger of them, Gabriel, decides to spontaneously lie in the well-kept lawn of one of the houses we are passing by. As he lies there, delighted to feel the soft grass bristle into his back, and as my older son joins him, the owner of the house comes out yelling profanities and holding a shotgun, threatening to shoot my young boys as trespassers. What would a reasonable reply on my part be like? I imagine that I would be incredulous, angry, and scared. I might yell "Are you serious?" as I rush to get my sons away from this lunatic. The implication in my question is the same as the misunderstanding of anyone who objects that education is not always serious. If this outrageous, gun-toting person were truly serious, she would never threaten the lives of two harmless children lying on her front lawn. She would recognize what is more important and would act *seriously* about it. When we see the things as they are, their reality is serious by ontological necessity. To be serious is simply to be faithful to what is the case, which may require a range of sentimental dispositions from sobriety to levity.

In other words, the objections from a teacher who feels that my construal of education as divinely serious might threaten the play and free time of school children underestimates what it is to be serious. She rightly understands that play and free time are very serious things. By doing so, she is asserting the seriousness of education present in the practice of playtime and daydreaming. This is the same variety of seriousness conveyed to a CEO by her doctor who orders her to go on a vacation in order to prevent a heart attack. Leisure can be serious. Education, in the very same way, is also serious. And this seriousness always begins and ends with the divine scent of life and death looming somewhere not too far away.

This objection has also created another problem. My reply could be misunderstood as asserting an axiological or prescriptive component to what education is. Let me be clear: I reject the distinction between "education" and "miseducation" as having to do with what education is. Real things are not good or evil; they simply are or are not the case. Education is not good or evil. It begins as something instead of nothing. Expecting an ontological analysis to render a thing real with the added dimension of being innocent or guilty, permissible or impermissible, is a mistake. For this reason, my use of Aristotle's notion of tragedy is intended to help reduce the reality of education away from the overly complicated normative prescriptions of ethics—as opposed to descriptions that end in art.

Moving from this non-axiological seriousness of education, we should consider the second Aristotelian dimension of tragedy: completeness. Education is complete because of its wholeness. Like the singularly plural universe that James believed in, education also has this complete aspect. To visualize this wholeness, think of bed linens: bed linens are whole because of their thread count. The tragic dimension of this wholeness is that nothing can be isolated or self-contained. As a whole, the parts become irreducible to the whole and cannot be divided. This wholeness adds to the mystery of education because we cannot separate it into parts without distorting its being-within Being. We cannot divide it into sterile subjects or lessons without losing the lifeblood that makes it complete in the first place. Education is wholly irreducible.

When we look at these two aspects together (seriousness and completeness) we find the third feature: possessing magnitude. It is a context. This brings us back to the "primal reality" of the divinity of education. The magnificence of education demands us to be serious about it as a complete whole. In the eyes of those who claim to see it, education possesses a breadth and depth that is as expansive as the mind, consciousness, and even life itself. Many call education something "lifelong" that verges on the eternal. Education possesses magnitude.

This Aristotelian trio (serious, complete, and possessing magnitude) is poetic, intended to describe art, and especially theatre. When we think of something beautiful, we find it has all of these features in one way or another. So, perhaps, we might also say that along with being divine and tragic, education is *beautifully* mysterious. The dark, overlapping hues of this description begin to outline the mysterious core of education. None of these colors contains moral or axiological statements. They simply are imagined statements of reality. In case this sounds strange or arrogant, here are some possible questions and answers:

Q: How does the mystery of education, in the ways you describe here, come to be the case?

A: Everything comes to be the case within the contextual world of Being. There are no alternatives to this.

Q: This may be true, but surely you do not think that you know what that world is or that your experience can totalize that world as such?

A: You are right. I do not think that.

Q: Then you must provide a better answer! How do these claims you have made come to be the case *to you*?

A: If you had asked that question, then I would have answered it. What I describe here concerning the mystery of education comes to be the case in the world of Being through impressions from my senses, intuitions, and desires that create beliefs in me about the way things are.

Q: Why are those beliefs and desires themselves the case universally, or at least generally—in a way that is worthwhile to and for a community of inquiry?

A: Because that is the way they seem to be at the moment to me. I speak of them as true because they are not yet untrue to me. Would you object to that? Would others you know object to this? Is not your objection itself an example of doing the same sort of thing?

Q: Is that all you can say?

A: Yes. I think so.

Q: So what was the point of all this?

ENCHANTING ABSENCE

In the final, unanswered question posed above, we find the pregnant gem of the divine, tragic, and perhaps even beautiful mystery that is education: frustrated desire. In it, we see the enchanting effect that mystery can have. We may even realize that a mystery lurks beneath everything. What is this effect? Mystery causes us to desire disclosure. Absence is full of erotic enchantment that frustratingly leads us to desire, with or without—and many times despite—volition, will, or intention. If we were to admit to the mystery that is education we would find this: Education as mystery reveals education as more, not less, desirable. If education were indeed in a crisis, as the politicians of schooling like to tell us, then the most basic reason for such a crisis would be because it has lost its appeal to us and we have lost our appetite for it. Or because we know that what is said to be Education is not serious enough to be real. A student who loves to fix cars or weld steel knows that taking practice tests for a standardized test is not education. How does something become more than just palatable? How do we make something so disenchanted desirable again? How do we recover desire for that which we are alienated from?

Let us imagine a more visible crisis of our time: starvation. Daily, thousands of people die of starvation around the world. Unlike an educational crisis, where appetite is lost, people who are starving long for food. The problem is simply one of feeding those who need food in the proper proportion. Education is different. An educational crisis reveals itself in the disfiguration of the desire itself and the subsequent loss of the object of desire in exchange for something—or nothing—else altogether. An educational crisis is more akin to obesity. In this case, we find that our desire for food continues but we desire food in a way that disenchants the very fact of what food is, the very reality of food. We even develop the desire to eat things that are not food at all to the most ordinary analysis, like reading the list of ingredients. Or, we celebrate "real food" as an exceptional spectacle.

Unlike ending starvation, where the desire for nourishment is still intact, educational problems point to an ontological confusion of desire: we no longer know what it is that we want and, consequently, we no longer *want to want* it. Again, this is not a moral or ethical issue. It is a failure of the ontological foundations of desire and action. The divine and tragic call of the mystery of education is largely seen as non-erotic and even unattractive. In its place we accept the ideology of Education and its fundamentalist certainties as a cheap substitute. Reacting against this, others have presented a world of pure, postmodern fiction, where nothing is real and everything is constructed by nothing. In both cases, when the thing at stake is obfuscated as perfectly certain or entirely fictional, we find a phenomenological crisis: the loss of the thing itself. The re-enchanting potential of mystery is this: in the positive absence that is the mystery of education we find a way to recover that thing we never had before: the reality of education, the mystery of education.

There are many examples and explanations that I might offer, but Disney sums them up in a saying I remember from my childhood in the animated adaptation of *Robin Hood*. In a scene that I can remember like it was yesterday, Maid Marian (the vixen) longs for Robin Hood (the fox). Her lady-in-waiting (the chicken) consoles her by quoting an English poet who wrote "Absence makes the heart grow fonder."

I find this chicken to be quite right. The power of a real and true absence is remarkably erotic and tragically powerful. (Think of the death of someone dearly beloved or the fate of star-crossed lovers.) When we feel the absence of the things we most deeply desire, we often experience a primal religious sensation that goes beyond generic belief or shallow intentions and into the realm of heartache, melancholia, and most radically, nostalgia for nostalgia: the longing for the home I've never had. What if we were to reimagine the mysterious reality of education as this very absence? What if the point of sustaining a reduction that reveals education as mystery was to re-enchant education as the undisclosed thing that *is*? How would we act about the politics of schooling once we admitted that the thing itself is too elusive to measure? What effect would this have on our actions and our lives?

Education as mystery has been described in many interwoven ways. It begins as a puzzling case: something difficult to figure out, like a detective novel. We also begin to see it as a way to combat the superstitious ideologies of the day. Here, education as mystery can be filtered through the lens of the school where we find the politics of the day and yesteryear and the psychological orientation of the art of teaching. Then, education as mystery can be understood as the seriousness we find analogous to the primal reality of the divine. This seriousness leads into the other Aristotelian dimensions of tragedy (completeness and wholeness) that also help to describe the mystery of education. And yet, it is not until we face the re-enchanting power of positive absence that we begin to see what mystery discloses by remaining undisclosed: the frustrating potency of education. This reality—the reality of the mystery of education—is itself still a mystery, as it should be. As such, we are challenged to face it and leave behind the urge to tame it by removing its most enchanting features. We should not want a domesticated, sterilized, disclosed, or fully revealed education for all the reasons that art can never be conquered or destroyed. We should want education that is from within the dark and wild flux of Being that James instructs us to face.

From the most opaque desires of the ontological quest for Being to the most practical needs of everyday action, the mystery of education rejects the relativistic neutrality of constructivist and postmodern epistemologies and simultaneously exposes the fundamentalist superstitions of Whiggish Puritanism and positivistic psychology. What is left is a real and true, divine and tragic, absent mystery that tells us what it is we long for when we desire the reality we hope to be education: the hope to become a human person. To be in relation, in ontological communion, to be-with, to dwell—even in relation to the unknown, the unknown forces and energies that drive us to study in our (un)conscious life.

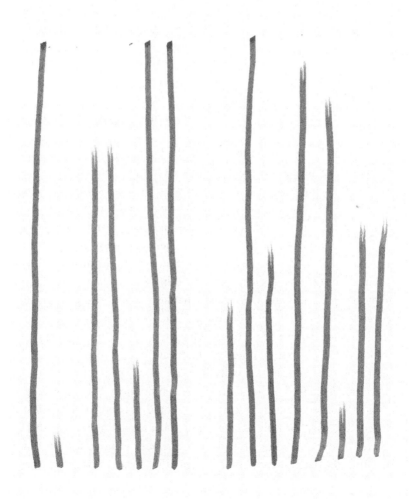

Four

The Eros of Study

My inability to study fills me with despair.

WILLIAM JAMES, *SELECTED UNPUBLISHED CORRESPONDENCE* 1885–1910

INTRODUCTION

How is it that the ability to study comes and goes, even as we long for it? If I desire to study, then (according to conventional wisdom) all that is left is for me to *do* it. In the schools of our day, "study!" is an often-heard command, and "study skills" are techniques to be acquired in remedial classes for the (supposedly) less able. In this chapter, I will investigate the ontology of study with the growing intuition that this conventional understanding of study in schools and elsewhere is misunderstood. Study cannot be a simple matter of intention, attention, or learning.[1] In addition, study must be associated with being within Being, subsisting, and existing. Study, as with most things, cannot be wholly determined by a strong will generated from a singular intending ego. If the reasons and examples provided are illuminating, then these two points should become apparent. First, volition does not rule the day when it comes to the art of study. Second, study subsists as an erotic force that comes and goes, but never leaves us altogether. In other

---

1. Here I use the term "intention" in its most ordinary form of expression and am not ignoring its more technical Husserlian sense of intentionality; nonetheless this chapter will ultimately address both volitional intention and the "object directedness" of intentionality.

words, despite our inability to execute it as a technique, study remains in our desire to do it. This not only contradicts convention, it also asserts the erotic dimension of study. Erotic study, then, is like other forms of eros: a wild thing, partly this and partly that, teeming with fortune.

To restate what I have said above: The analysis in this chapter should begin to reveal study as less intentional than the common view that takes it to be paying voluntary attention to something for an extended amount of time—with corresponding results lurking right behind, and definite prescriptive things to say. It should also show how the orthodox phenomenological understanding of intentionality places an ontological burden upon consciousness that may be misleading, although it does establish a non-psychologistic understanding of objects. Emerging from this erotic theory of study, then, we might also begin to see a corrective suggestion to phenomenological approaches that rely on intentionality as the primary or sole force of reduction and replace it (intentionality) with the complexities of subsistence. In place of purely intentional accounts of study (which are not the same as the notion of intentionality), I will describe study that subsists erotically, that lives in and through desire, but also within a subsistent ecology of fortune. Unlike the idea that erotic desire is itself willed into being, a closer reduction should discover that eros, like study, simply subsists. This location of erotic study in the category of subsistence will shift and clarify the ontological geography of the trinitarian lens from the outer-place of Being, into the middle-place of subsistence.

Because of this shift, the conceptual geography should begin to appear more concretely and in better proportion. Unlike the dark, but positive, absence of education described in the previous chapter on Being, the eros of study should be easier to see than the overwhelming vastness of Being that leaves us blind and dumbfounded. Study seems to be more (using "more" as an ontological quantification) than the general sense of the context of Being, where we seek but do not find education. Thus, the erotic subsistence of study will continue to describe this particular place within our lens: the ontological category of subsistence, the place where forces and energies of life and death mediate between Being and existence—the category of ghostly things that live between existence and Being. This is why we should expect to have more sensory places to look for and discuss study than we had while investigating education.

For this reason, this chapter is not only descriptive. It is also the best space to convey the general contours of my phenomenological instrument, the trinitarian lens. In other words, since subsistence lives between Being and existence, we will need to identify it in relation to its outer and inner categories, rather than try to locate it statically on its own. In sections to follow, the descriptive terms map on to the ontological categories in this way:

Being, subsistence, and existence

Once again, the question at hand is ontological: What is study? My reply will be that study "is" in one sense and "is not" in another sense. It "is" insofar as it must be something in the world, between Being and existence. It "is not" insofar as it is not Being or existence; instead, it subsists uniquely in the region where we find life forces that drive things in the world. In the sections to follow, I will present my reasons for these statements.

PHYSIOPSYCHOLOGY

The first consideration for this investigation will begin with what we know from existence and move outwards towards subsistence. In other words, we will begin with the body as a site of recognition and move from it towards consciousness. This is not an original approach. James's psychological descriptions in his *Principles* are largely based on the empirical, material observations of the brain and its nervous tissue.[2] At the same time, this phenomenological approach to psychology does not require orthodoxy to a particular author or school of psychology. We do not need to do as James did and delve into anatomical physiology *per se* to see the surface of what I am referring to as "physiopsychology."

Physiopsychology points to this basic expectation: the physical body, the subject of anatomy and physiology, has *something* to do with psychology, the life of the mind and consciousness.[3] If this expectation seems reasonable, then consider these two explanations, one in the negative and the other positive:

> The *explanation from death* is that a physical assault on the body, an action that abuses it to the point of murdering it, is not unrelated to being alive. Furthermore, this physiological life that is threatened by physical force is not unrelated to the psychological life of consciousness.

> The *explanation from life* is more revealing. In order for our body to survive and stay alive—to subsist, in other words—many different things have to be simultaneously present. This simultaneous presence

2. See, for example, this passage where James invites his reader to join him in observing the physical and physiological aspects of the brain: "Nothing is easier than to familiarize oneself with the mammalian brain. Get a sheep's head, a small saw, chisel, scalpel and forceps (all three can best be had from a surgical instrument maker), and unravel its parts either by the aid of a human dissecting book, such as Holden's *Manual of Anatomy*, or by the specific direction *ad hoc* given in such books as Foster and Langley's *Practical Physiology* (Macmillan) or Morrell's *Comparative Anatomy and Dissection of Mammalia* (Longmans)." *Principles*, 7.

3. If anyone were to dispute this meta-assumption, then they could easily find it in more detail in the opening chapter of James's *Principles*. There he presents his opening theories of psychology relying on a "cerebralist" approach that is vividly captured in his description of "plasticity," where he writes: "Organic matter, especially nervous tissue, seems endowed with a very extraordinary degree of plasticity of this sort; so that we may without hesitation lay down as our first proposition the following, that the phenomena of habit in living bodies are due to the plasticity of the organic materials of which their bodies are composed" (68).

of things might even begin to describe what life is. At the very least, it gives a minimal description of what the live body is: a thing that subsists, a dynamic thing teeming with innumerably different forces and energies simultaneously and actively present.

This vital presence can be altered in directly intended ways: when we move the body parts that we think we can control (such as when I move my arms and legs), when we use the body to cause an effect on the body (such as when I exercise to lose weight), or when we allow the body be in a position to be influenced (such as when I stand out in the cold). Nonetheless, however much we can direct our bodies with certain amounts of clearly felt intention, the vast proportion of our bodily life-presence is out of our hands when we intend for it to respond to the stimulus of intention. After repeated intentional actions (such as typing on a keyboard) we usually begin to perform the same body-actions without the aspect of strong intention. After a certain amount of time, we might call these things "habits." The most habitual body-actions (like our heartbeat), of course, are completely out of our control in the immediate function; even as we tend think ourselves in complete possession of "our" body. There is a strange gap between my existence and the subsistent forces and processes that keep me alive.

Our bodies often seem to have multiple minds of their own; they possess competing interests and abilities. We ignore the strong opinions of our bodies (such as extreme pain) at our peril, but the weak opinions (such as minor pleasures and discomforts) go beyond our ability to respond to, or even realize, intentionally. We cannot pay attention to everything that happens in and to our bodies. Even when we seem to take deliberate forms of action on behalf of our bodies (such as taking medicine), the results are very unpredictable for a variety of known and unknown reasons, and always rely on degrees of probability. It is true that finding harmony with one's own body—the needs, desires, and whims of bodily subsistence and existence—is a lifelong project that always ends in failure: death.

Therefore, because the negative evidence (the explanation from death) reveals that the body is not irrelevant to our overall conscious life, and the positive evidence (the explanation from life) shows that much of the life of the human organism is involuntary, then, physiopsychology teaches us this lesson: *being alive, or subsisting, is not purely or primarily voluntary.* There is no equivalence between our existence and our subsistence. Voluntary intention is a proportionally small, secondary, and unreliable part of our physiopsychic life. I make this claim because even the body, which I take as a phenomenological first instance from existence, operates in its own times, spaces, and manners. It even has its own reasons, and the most absurd to us is its final decision to perish. I assume that this descriptive, existential case offers us an ontological suggestion about subsistence: things cannot be altogether different from our physiopsychological ways of subsisting without betraying an infidelity to reality.

This should not be confused with an attempt to advance a *purely* deterministic theory of life. Even the ever-skeptical James declared that his first act of free will was to believe in free will. Whether we will admit it or not, we must believe (albeit skeptically for some) that we have the capacity to deliberately will *some* things and hope for the best. But, even when we are convinced that we have a recipe for success, we can and do fail for reasons that are all too often mysterious.

Some would call this an acknowledgment of the unconscious, and that would not be incorrect. However, in order to ask as little as possible from your intuitions, and my own, I am not asking that you submit the entirety of subsistence to an abstract unconscious. I am always a bit unsure of what to make of psychoanalytic language that speaks consciously about the unconscious. After all, whatever could be understood as "unconscious" would be a part of consciousness by the basic assumption described here: even the unconscious is not disembodied. If I am unconscious then I am such a thing in *this* body, over here, not that one sitting over there. I subsist as *me* insofar as I subsist in *this* particular existential space of flesh and bone that I call "my body."

For these reasons, physiopsychology is relevant to our ongoing investigation of the ontology of study within the category of subsistence.[4]

---

4. To remain faithful to the minimalism required by phenomenological reduction (as described in ch. 2), this description is made with no "supporting" scholarship. However, two of the already cited authors present more developed studies that support the claims I make in this section. In Warnick's *Education and Imitation* (see ch. 2) the question of becoming is premised on the fact that imitative processes happen involuntarily. Along with psychological literature, Warnick also delves into cognitive science that verifies the existence of a vast unconscious life in human beings. The most expansive source, of course, is William James. In many places James makes a nuanced case for the primacy of involuntary attention in the human will. Most direct are his sections on "Attention" and "Will" in his *Principles* and reprinted in *Psychology: A Briefer Course*. The most famous theories of this sort, of course, come out of the vast resources of psychoanalysis—with which I am mostly unfamiliar. However, as this section argues, one need not make an uninformed psychoanalytic leap to see the skeletal aspects of my point here.

CONSCIOUSNESS AND SUBSISTENCE

Physiopsychology is observed through the body and yet this is not an existential observation in the strictest sense (that view is reserved for the following chapter). This is an important point to keep in mind. It should begin to clarify the *relationships* between the organizing categories (Being, subsistence, and existence) that constitute the phenomenological tool for this project: the trinitarian lens. Since subsistence mediates between Being and existence, it, in turn, can best be seen through the *relationship* between Being and existence, which is simply to reserve a space for the things that we find in between the two categories and reserve them descriptive integrity.

Whereas the previous chapter reasoned from the mystery of the world of Being, this chapter begins to move from the vast world of being towards the human person (the subject of the next chapter) and the material universe. Between these two behemoths—Being and existence, the world and the universe—we find the intermediary space of subsistence. If we pay attention to its unique location, we might begin to see the ontological geography of consciousness and the role of fortune and chance. In other words, there is an intimate spatial relationship between the subject matter of psychology (what James calls the "science of the mind's laws" and what I refer to here as the phenomenon of "consciousness") and the ontological category of subsistence.

The relationship between these two things could justifiably raise a great deal of speculation as to the *exact* nature of these relations. Sadly, I cannot remark on that question here. My interest is only directed at the question of what study is within this general conceptual geography. That is to say this: Whereas the vast mystery of education within Being lent itself (in chapter 3) to forms of ontological and even religious speculation, the subsistence of study lends itself to physiopsychological speculation. Unlike psychological theories and methods that take for granted the ontological location of consciousness, whatever psychology this might be must begin by noting the distinct, subsistent space of consciousness. The role that consciousness (and study) plays, then, is to mediate between what exists and what Is; to remind my existence here is to recall itself within Being with the reflexivity of analyzing the recollection itself within subsistence. In this view, I suspect that my understanding of consciousness might part company with my mentor William James. A further departure, noted in the previous chapter, is that education is placed beyond the realm of consciousness. In other words, "educational psychology" is an incoherent terminology for this analysis; only a "psychology of study" is relevant here. Regardless of that issue of nomenclature, the reasons for the departure mentioned are embedded in the phenomenological method I have laid out, but are not the primary objective of this book.

THE FUNDAMENTALITY OF FORTUNE

A second reason for proposing a corrective theory of study can be understood by reversing the methodological direction of the section on physiophychology. Instead of moving from existence to subsistence, from the physiological to the psychological, we might see what going from Being to subsistence will do. Referring again to the ontological categories, instead of the direction of *existence » subsistence* in the section on physiophychology, this section will reverse the polarity and move in this way: *subsistence «* *Being*. This reversal reveals a dialectic between two radically different ontological categories. This takes us past the physiopsychological move into the world at large, with the same ontological order and rationale.

I begin with this expectation: The excessive world of Being has *something* to do with subsistence. This minimal expectation is clarified, again, in these similar, yet modified, explanations:

> The *explanation from death* asserts that just as an assault on an existing body is not irrelevant to subsisting, so too it is with the world. Nihilism or ontological nothingness, the complete annihilation of Being, is not irrelevant to subsistence. In other words, the world of Being is not irrelevant to the task of surviving it.

> The *explanation from life* is less demanding. In order to survive in the world, living things—subsisting things, in other words—must subsist in a way that is not unlike the world of Being itself. Life forces cannot escape or divorce themselves from Being nor can they be rightly understood as Being itself. They must subsist in a contingent way within Being. When viewed from this perspective, we begin to see something like what has been called the "life-world," an energetic backdrop that presupposes a world to support it.

Considering these two proofs in relation to the world will require descriptions not unlike the physiopsychological ones offered in the earlier section. To do so, consider the distinction between the following contrasting terms used to describe both the world and the life—even psychological life—we find in it: *Fortune* and *nonfortune*.

Fortune is an ontological designation, not an axiomatic or moral one. When I wish someone I love "fortune" I am wishing that person "*good* fortune." This is what I mean when I tell my family, "Wish me luck!": I am asking for *good* luck, not just any kind of luck. On its own, however, fortune (and its synonym "luck") simply subsists—nothing more, nothing less. Lady Fortuna is not an ethical superstition. She really and truly is unpredictable and unshakable. In *After Virtue*, Alasdair MacIntyre describes her as "that bitch-goddess of unpredictability," and goes on to say, "we cannot dethrone her."[5] A fortunate life, then, is neither good nor bad on its own. It just is as it is. There is no disputing it: fortune can only be suffered.

For this reason, *nonfortune* is not the same as *mis*fortune. Misfortune is merely *about* fortune. Nonfortune is itself a different thing. Whereas misfortune implies something like a bad influence, nonfortune fundamentally lacks the ontology we find in fortune. Like fortune, nonfortune is not a good or bad, healthy or ill thing on its own. It simply lacks the ontological vulnerability to chance and randomness. Literally, nonfortune is *not* fortune. Therefore, a nonfortunate life is the most radical opposite of a fortunate one. Nonfortune recasts the world in the image of a strange otherworldliness: predictability, certainty, and the exile of chance.

The effect we might imagine of such a life would be a sense of the world, and an approach to it that would be quintessentially superstitious and deterministic. In other words, it would rely on things that are not in the world to determine worldly outcomes. Like a person who sees tarot cards, astrological signs, or test scores as reliable reasons to feel secure about things and predicates wagers based on them, so too with nonfortune: It is certain to subvert the ontological uncertainty of fortune with certainty. It is an attempt to sterilize beauty to the very edge of annihilation. Nonfortune is nihilistic; it threatens more than subsistence; it threatens everything.

Anyone who denies fortune and endorses nonfortune outright could only do so for reasons that would be extremely hard to imagine and intuit as beautiful, real, or true. It may be the case that some might seek consolation by pretending to escape the fortune of reality altogether, but even they must at some point admit to this strategic coping mechanism. While this may only be a failure of my own imagination, I suspect it is more than that. Perhaps it is so difficult to imagine someone rejecting fortune because nonfortune is

5. MacIntyre, *After Virtue*, 94.

sterile. As far as I know, there is no place in the world where things are really and truly predictable from the bottom up (or the top down). Everything is filled with things that escape and later might surprise, delight, or terrorize us. As pointed out in the previous chapter, even if someone holding to a nonfortunate view would admit to a certain amount of chance in things, she would nonetheless argue that the fortunate side of things is proportionally miniscule and unimportant when compared to the nonfortunate one, or that there is a great deal of progress being made in the abolition of fortune.

This strange ideological superstition is an attempt to guard against the inevitable winds of fortune. Yet, the hubris of nonfortune is not a moral lesson; it is an ontological reminder of the fortune of nonfortune. Even in the face of claims to certainty and demands for accountability there are still ghostly whispers of death, fear of the unknown, and wonder about the beginning of time. In those ghostly voices we begin to realize that nonfortune is only the case because fortune begets it. It is fantasy created by fortune, and it is a (kind of) response, but it cannot call from itself. Nonfortune has no voice. Without the immovability of fortune in the world there would be no fearful reasons to want to tame or escape it. Nonfortune is a defensive thesis that, to the person who endorses it, may seem to hold on to things that are true and real, but in doing so, nonfortune distorts the vulnerability of the world. It cages the wildness and fertility of things out of fear of the unknown. Nonfortune has no future because the future is always fortunate.

For these reasons, nonfortunate certainty could never be called foundational or universal. After all, if there were anything that we could reliably regard as foundational and universal, it would be the *unreliability* of things.[6] It is fortune, then—not nonfortune—that presents a world that is sufficiently unpredictable to be called foundational and universal. Despite this reliable unreliability of things, nonfortunate theories abound. Theory itself, when allowed to escape ontological fundamentals, is nonfortunate, no matter what its specific epistemological content might be about.

Even in the face of the grand randomness of science after Darwin, Einstein, Gödel, and Heisenberg, among others, there is a disturbing trend to see a particularly nonfortunate form of scientific rationality as a way to neutralize or eradicate fortune altogether in social institutions. In schools, this is apparent in the proliferation of standardized testing. Standardized tests are considered to be effective ways to domesticate the wild mystery of

6. This is, as I see it, the magnificent genius of Darwin's insight into natural selection: there is nothing "natural" about it.

education with "science." (And, in many ways, they are.) Supposedly this ontological castration that decouples things from the world, knowing from knowing-about, will produce effects that vindicate the messianic Gospel of Schoolvation, and its sponsor, the nation-state. Invariably, it contributes to my description of contemporary schooling in the previous chapter as predominantly, and problematically, superstitious.[7]

It is for this reason that the dialectic between fortune and nonfortune should be revealing to this study of study: While the sometimes-overestimated "testing taboo" is well known these days—but all too often ignored by policy makers, to be sure—it is the *preparation* for these superstitious and nonfortunate tests that should be equally alarming to us for ontological, not moral, reasons.

Thus, physiopsychology and the fundamentality of fortune bring us to the ontological question of the subsistence of study: taking into account the physiopsychology of the human person and the fundamentality of fortune in the world of Being, what, then, is study?

THE SIGNS OF CONVENTION

Before offering concrete examples, a potential misunderstanding should be clarified. However critical I have been about and toward what has been referred to as the "conventional view" of study, this critique should not be taken too far, especially since my reasoning is largely based upon conventional, intuitive ways of thinking. It would be unwise to think that all convention is useless in this matter. Ontological objections do not so much rail against convention pure and simple. Instead of the facility of decrying convention, a worthwhile ontological critique should also be able to point out that the thing taken to be "conventional" is not sufficiently conventional or *thingly* to be taken at face value. It cannot deface things gratuitously. It can only *demask* to reveal the potentiality of a face.

For this reason, I think that there are many aspects of study within the conventions of schooling that hold rich signs of a deeper and more

---

7. In the preface to his volume *Theologico-Political Treatise*, Benedict de Spinoza expresses this now-common view of the relationship between superstition and fortune: "Men would never be superstitious, if they could govern all their circumstances by set rules, or if they were always favored by fortune: but being frequently driven into straits where rules are useless, and being often kept fluctuating pitiably between hope and fear by the uncertainty of fortune's greedily coveted favours, they are consequently, for the most part, very prone to credulity." *Chief Works of Benedict de Spinoza*, 1:3.

real sense of study, embedded in the poverty of "practice tests" and "study skills." I have seen, time and time again, a disfigured thing that still holds fundamental signs that remind me that the thing in question is still there, at least in potentiality, despite how totally hidden it may seem to me. It goes without saying that the subtle signs of repugnant things do not—and should not—refute their conventional expressions. A thing can never depart from itself entirely. For this reason, no matter how deformed and disenchanted they may be, the conventions of study are not to be discarded *in toto*. In fact, many of their subtle signs might be in need of radical recovery.

Keeping that view in mind, allow me to present two examples where I think we can see the erotic subsistence of study. As I move along, there will be many parts to these exemplars that mirror the conventions we find in the scientific testing of schools. These signs are rich and useful to us, not troublesome or contradictory. Most notably, we will find practices of preparation through memory and repetition that apply to both the ideal and its more common reality. In my view, none of these fairly conventional aspects of study should be abandoned as practices; they need to be seen as more than cheap masquerades. They need to be reimagined and re-enchanted through a trinitarian lens. That is what, in my view, the examples to follow possess that "study skills classes" lack. It is also what we find in James's despair (noted in the epigraph to this chapter) on the occasion when he deceives us into thinking that he cannot study.

BABY-TALK AND JAZZ

Babies and jazz musicians have a lot in common. They are both trying to say something. Their ways of speaking, however, subsist because they do not exist: they are simultaneously preparatory and performative. It is this unity of preparation and performance that sets them apart as articulate examples of what I mean here by the eros of study. Before illustrating what I mean in the examples themselves, consider this preliminary formulation: *study is an erotic subsistent force that allows no distinction between preparation and performance.*

Baby-talk. Years before formal instruction, toddlers begin to acquire speech. There are wide variations from child to child, but certain aspects seem to be fairly constant. To begin with, long before formal speaking and imitative word-associations, and even before the earliest mimicry of infantile *echolalia*, there are purely acoustic prerequisites:

bare vocal noise and sounds. A sign of life in a delivery room is a good, loud cry. Noise is also a sign that infants have the potential to vocalize speech. Without the ability to acoustically make vocal noise, vocal speech is impossible, although the possibility for language remains. Perhaps this is the reason why it is common for infants to vocalize at random for unexplainable reasons. It often seems, at least to me, that these noises—low intonations, high intonations, rapid stuttering using the tongue or the hand, strong yells in echo-prone places, and more—are fascinating and experimental. This much seems to be true about baby-talk: it happens between Being and existence. It verifies the earliest, ontological, and unconscious "Am" of a person and mediates between that and the existential "*I* am."

This acoustic proto-speech is an instance in which we can witness the eros of study within the ontological category of subsistence. We can sense study during these sacred moments of infantile vocal experimentation. Prior to the event of speech and the ordering of language, there is a strange thing that happens with no direct instruction or technique and very questionable rationality and even self-consciousness. There is nothing other than what seems to be there to begin with. What is this first-thing? The least we can say is eros. This is not the excess of the mysterious world of Being, this is the erotic force of subsistence that we cannot see, but we can sense.

Jazz. Consider another, more developed, example: Mastering an instrument. In this case, the guitar. I want to focus on the mastery-end of the spectrum in this example to show that the eros of study are not only to be found in the earliest moments of life, in both the qualitative and the quantitative sense of longevity. Much like the effortless experimentations of a noise-making infant, a master guitarist plays with an organic wildness that is the hallmark of the craft. Without this wild, effortless character, this so-called master is discovered to be a fraud. And as much as it may seem that this mastery is gained from a self-directed program and routine of practice—which most certainly is a vital *part* of the process—the master will most likely describe the experience in reverse order. Spending years of repetition, imitation, and experimentation on the physical space of a guitar's neck, body, strings, frets, and so much more—using the finite limits of physical dexterity and technique, all the while remaining constantly in-process, never finished, yet extremely proficient and confident—is not to try to *possess* the instrument as a generic machine, nor as a particular crafted piece of wood, glue, and steel. A master guitarist is not trying to domesticate her guitar. This is why "mastery" is a misleading term. It is not so much that an expert guitarist has *mastered* the instrument, but that the instrument and the artist have become one, or perhaps something altogether beyond the master-slave dialectic. Communion: a true master of any instrument would likely describe the process as being possessed by something else, beyond the finitude of the person or the instrument, something not entirely physical nor anything too remote: an intense desire for rich, communal love; a genetic curiosity about melodic, rhythmic, and harmonic colors and shapes; a religious thirst for beauty and many other things that subsist.

To "study" guitar in this way is not to simply take lessons. Many guitar masters never took lessons. Wes Montgomery never did. To study is more properly understood as to never stop taking lessons from everything, and to simultaneously perform and prepare during these abundant lessons. This may sound opaque, but if you listen to a master musician warm up, you will hear the simplest practice scales performed beautifully. The expectant chaos of a tuning orchestra is not the same thing as the ear-grinding wails of an amateur violinist. The music that guides a master guitarist is not a score or a sheet; instead, it could be anything. While playing the guitar, an instrument that you cradle in your arms, like a child, the master guitarist cannot take that intimate posture for granted. It is said that Segovia once spoke these words: "Lean your body forward slightly to support the guitar against your chest, for the poetry of the music should resound in your heart." The master guitarist never studies in the cold, isolated sense of routine practicing. At the same time, the master guitarist is always at study—a thick, warm, erotic, and endless form of study—even when the instrument is in its case and someone (or something) else's music plays.

To be more concrete and less presumptuous, let us look to the bare process of what happens. When a song is played, any decent player can attest to this fact: what we call "music" is the product of a relational event where the player, the instrument, and the context itself—the other musicians, others who might be present and/or listening, the acoustics of the room, a muse, the ghosts of memories and nostalgia for nostalgia—become one thing. In a more radical way, whenever the score is not predetermined, such as in jazz improvisation, we find that there is no line dividing the preparation from the performance. In a jazz soloist's work, we can literally see and hear, as in the infant mentioned before, the eros of study. I say this for the following reasons: in order to solo over a set of melodic and rhythmic changes, or even over a single, continuous note and rhythm (a "vamp" is the musical term)—or, even more radical still, over nothing at all—a jazz soloist cannot play willfully extracted memories from a previous lesson or isolated repetitions that are somehow disconnected to the past or present, with no future direction. If she did, her performance would be exposed as an amateurish façade. She relies on a thicker memory that is the sum total of things voluntary and involuntary, determined and free, that she has accumulated and somehow remembered—even if for the very first time. She is doing something that cannot be learned but must be acquired and can never be bought or sold and many times can only be offered. She makes an offering.

She repeats things that simply are the case to her imagination because she has been immersed in them for so long that they are present to her, even present in a dark past or a blurry future. Like a chef's seasoning, she does not look at her instrument to measure out what she is doing. Her eyes are closed. She does not deliberate even when she waits and shows patience. Often there is no time to do so. She imagines and plays in a stroke. Sometimes, she plays nothing at all. Other times, she plays every note she can find—even ones that have never existed before. If she is right-handed, then, her right hand's fingers strike, pick, or pluck this string and then that one, in this and/or that certain way, according to this and/or that sense of rhythm, sometimes one at a time, other times in bold strokes or careful bunches, all depending on what she imagines and what the music requires to be itself, to be beautiful, to show by offering. The fingers on her left hand go from this fret to this other one, or rest in clusters together on different strings and frets (or on different strings on the same fret) to form chords, or leave the strings open; all of it in a fit of expression that is as new as it is old, as deliberate as it is random, as preparatory as it is performative. And this is just the beginning of the options: there are slides, e-bows, real bows, saltshakers, and picks and pennies and acrylic fingernails to choose from.

Whether she is willing to believe it or not, the form of life that sustains this rich experience requires the full consideration of the voluntary and the involuntary with the constant variable of fortune always in and around it. By the way: This is not all to be found under dim lights and critical acclaim. Most of it is located in a rehearsal studio, a living room, or even in a daydream.

Baby-talk as jazz. The artist—a cooing baby, the master guitarist, a curious physicist, the passionate teacher, a confused student, the tragic lover—each knows about the subsistence of erotic study because, like Zarathustra, she can understand that "Higher than love of the neighbor is love of the farthest and the future"; and declare with him, "higher yet than the love of the human beings I esteem the love of things and ghosts."[8] The eros of study, then, is found in a jazz guitarist's solo because it, too, like baby-talk, can only come from those who are willing to love that ghostly thing, eros, to sense its presence and let it show. And the love that this love begets reveals the human person at study. We know this for reasons unexplainable and mysterious to us (after all, they dwell within Being) but we can say this much: the eros of study cannot be either prepared or performed. It is always a preparation *and* a performance.

MEMORY AND REPETITION

What these two examples display is not exceptional to the conventions we find in study. They are not beyond the everyday. Just the opposite: they are entirely ordinary. These may be exceptions in the sense that they locate two uniquely situated places on polar sides of a life cycle, but they do not dwell there with any exclusivity. The point of considering the two poles, from infancy to mastery, is precisely to show this breadth of coverage.

The acquisition of memory through repetition is an ordinary and common trait of study. And for good reason: it works. That fact alone—the fact that memorization and repetition work—is a cautionary tale to not reinvent the wheel. If we take this warning to heart, then, alluding to the ontological contours of the eros of study would be insufficient on its own. I must explain how this eros function without throwing away the baby with the bathwater, so to speak. At the same time, the link between memory and conscious intent should remain loose and shaky.

It would be a reactionary mistake to think that this erotic notion of study absolves the person from the need to do anything or that it gives license to do everything. At the same time, as I argued earlier, it is also too simplistic to think that study can happen through a naïve gesture of voluntary intentionality. So, as with most things, the answer lies somewhere else.

8. Nietzsche, *Thus Spoke Zarathustra*, 173.

Although I would not go as far as to call this alternative a "middle way," it does seem to recover what is true in both directions. To account for the eros of study requires a more rigorous consideration of memory and repetition.

Memory. We find that "remembering" something can be quite different from "memorizing" it. I can try to remember where I left my keys or I can experience memory by remembering something at random. I can even remember things that I desire to *not* remember, or things I am not sure whether I have remembered or imagined for the very first time. Memorization, on the other hand, is not as multifunctional. And yet, there are times when knowing something by heart requires memorization. When we put aside semantics and move beyond this word or that one, I think we can begin to see that memory, in all its facets, is a thick thing that bears all the complexities of our bodies, consciousness, and the world. For this reason, the eros of study does not abandon memory and counter-memory. Instead, study thickens up recollection and remembrance; it heals and wounds, reminds, consoles and ruins. We need to remember things through both our exercises of will and from the depths of our repressed and unconscious knowledge that goes as deep as the imagination itself and the life it draws from. As described in the scenario of the jazz guitarist, we remember by subsisting through Being, our bodies, our minds, our souls, our desires, the fortune of the real.

The distinction between short- and long-term memory is basic enough, yet both forms of memory assume that memory is an external act of memorization. The eros of study does not favor short or long-term memory because they both miss the mark. To remember something richly is fundamentally unquantifiable, and deeply erotic, laden with desire. In fact, the memories that stay with us are usually those that have the unique aspect of awakening our desires. The cultivation of a thick memory, then, is also through the usual process: repetition.

Repetition. The world is on repeat. Repetition is the norm, not the exception. Things repeat, however unrepeatable those repetitions may be. For this reason, to repeat oneself is something we do all the time. We constantly repeat ourselves, which is one reason why from year to year we are mostly recognizable to others. The world is repetitive too, as all theories of eternal recurrence show. Although each repetition is uniquely situated, there is something repetitious about it nonetheless. Consequently, the grand sum of repetitions is a large portion of what we remember or recall. Other times, it is the *contrast* to the normative repetition of things that raises something to the surface of our memory. I will never forget when I saw mountains for the first time: they literally went above the surface of what I was used to repeating itself in my topographic vision of things. Despite this ever-presence of repetition, many treat it as exceptional instead of normal. This, as I see it, is an ontological mistake.

It is this link between a thick memory and normal repetition that seems to distinguish the eros of study from conventional notions of study. While they both carry many of the same signs, the eros of study express a more accurate ontology—an ontology that sees the physiopsychological human person and seeks the fortune of the world where the mystery of education abides. When we cultivate a thick memory within the normal of repetition, we realize that in the end, *study is beyond our control.* For this reason, James's despair is both more complex and more instructive to us than we might think.

Despite his "inability to study," James's despair is potent with study, with his desire for it and the ghostly desire of study for him. The erotics of study reveal what it is to be studious, as opposed to studying in a given moment or instance. It is this poignant despair, expressed in the epigraph, during the exercise of letter-writing, which has guided this chapter's study of study. In short, there is no convention that can escape eros. Like the subsistent force of gravity, the eros of study subsists and offer a way to exist within Being without forgetting the ghostly forces that push and pull and join the trinitarian refrain. The subsistence of study offers us more than the cosmic mystery of education but less than the embodied existence of the human person. The eros of study mediates between the human person and the world through the particular ontological passion that calls from beyond and within.

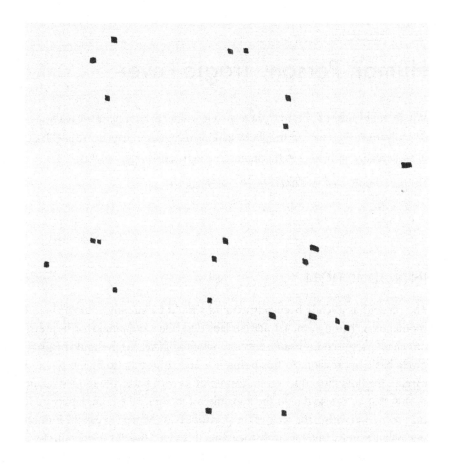

Five

Human Person, Tragic Lover

Where would any of *us* be, were there no one willing to know us as we really are or ready to repay us for *our* insight by making recognizant return? We ought, all of us, to realize each other in this intense, pathetic, and important way.

WILLIAM JAMES, *WHAT MAKES A LIFE SIGNIFICANT*

INTRODUCTION

The object has already been pushed and should be gaining some heat and momentum. Through the trinitarian lens described and employed in previous chapters, the contours of a developing ontological sketch should begin to give a basic impression. At this point, it is also important to be modest and careful, to allow the reduction to simmer at its own pace. The modest scope of this chapter is also due to the enormity of its topic: the human person. It may seem odd within the scale of the previous two chapters to call the human person enormous, but, relatively speaking, this topic dwarfs the previous two. After all, it is not controversial to note that, especially since Descartes, and perhaps since Augustine, our favorite topic of discussion has been ourselves. And there is little doubt that the question of the generic person, and all of its other nomenclatures, is among the thorniest of philosophy.

I am aware that there is a great deal of interest in what is today called "post-humanism" or even "anti-humanism," and in some cases I find sympathy for facets of such views, but my patience is tested when the irony of this sort of talk goes unaccounted for. Only humans could come up with an idea like post- or anti-humanism, because there are few things more quintessentially human than these sorts of ideas. Indeed, there is nothing quite as Cartesian, if one actually reads the *Meditations*, than many of the popular and cheap critiques of Cartesian rationality that abound in the post-postmodern academy today. And yet, humanism is itself a very particular doctrine that contains much more than the ordinary language of humanity, and it is that tradition and discourse that is often critiqued in traditions like post-modernism and post-structuralism. No one except a philosopher could deny that philosophy is, in a very particular sense, fundamentally anthropological (which is not to say anthropocentric). And as difficult as the questions surrounding the human person might be for philosophy, philosophers are not the only ones positing serious responses. Nor are they suggesting the best responses.

This chapter will provide directions for further reading and contemplation—reading and contemplation that, if their content is chewed slowly enough, might begin to help us digest the overall project and its implications for things, especially for a distinctly personalist sense of the art of teaching, guided by the subsistence of study and the *mysterium tremendum* of education described earlier. I also hope to show that it is a mistake to think of a school as being public prior to admitting to the public nature of the human person. Indeed, without a public conception of the human person there is no sense to imagining politics or anything public at all.

WHY THE HUMAN PERSON?

I use the expression "human person" to add precision and limit possible notions of personhood writ large. A *human* person implies that there are nonhuman persons. This is at least plausible from two directions: an ecological and a theological view of personhood. The ecological view of personhood sees animals and other animate beings as nonhuman persons; the theological view recognizes celestial and divine beings as nonhuman persons. Of course, these two directions find mutual expressions in many cases, such as the Franciscan tradition, and many would dismiss both as well. But it is out of respect for each view, individually and as a whole, that I refer to the *human* person, and not to the person in a generic and imprecise way. At the same time, it would be a category mistake to assume that my inclusion of the term "human" into the expression "human person" is an attempt to use the word *theoretically*, referring to some form of humanism or caricature of anthropocentrism. I am agnostic about the term in that sense; I only use it as a qualifier. In section Latin and Greek, "Person" and Person, however, I will treat the term "person" without the qualifier, for clarity of expression.

THE RELIGIOUS SIGNIFICANCE OF THE QUESTION

"Ask an educated European today what his thoughts are when one uses the term 'human being' [der Mensch], and he will just about always find three irreconcilable ideas about the term, which are in continuous conflict with each other."[1] That is how Max Scheler opens his insightful book *The Human Place in the Cosmos*, published a year before his death in 1928. Not much has changed. Disputes abound regarding the different terms used to refer to the particular space inhabited by these "human" bodies and their various aspects that make them into persons.[2] Person, Subject, Self, Human, Man, Ego, all locate sites of controversy, and often overspecialized theoretical terminology. This is mostly for good reason, especially since many of the theoretical disputes acquire their terms slowly and rigorously. However, all such disputes ultimately happen in the first person. In other words, the speaker tends to see herself as the thing at stake. What is not very easily disputed is the *existence* of human persons, ontologically speaking, within Being and subsistence. This is the continuity from Augustine to Descartes to my son Tomas's objection to being called a goose.

We find that amidst the controversy—the many genealogical myths to be found and the hermeneutic twists and turns of language, for instance— existence, like Being, has the qualities of *Vorgefundenes* (the-thing-that-has-been-there-before), at a more intimate location for anyone who can read these words. It may be the case that since Being appears with or without subsistence and existence inside of it, then the existing human person is an ontological option to Being, not a necessity. But, if we look closer, I would suggest that the aspect of the human person both in the world of Being and the life-world of subsistence is also unique to Being and might not be so easily removed from it. In effect, the human person is revealed in

---

1. Scheler, *Human Place in the Cosmos*, 5.

2. A good example of this is Abraham Heschel's brief text *Who Is Man?* There are many other texts, more than I could possibly mention here, and several of them will be treated in some detail as I move along.

the ways that, as James suggests in the epigraph to this chapter, are "intense, pathetic, and important."

In particular, we find that the "human person," in all of its semantic variation, conveys very different senses, with serious ontological questions at stake, depending on its inflections and variations, even if we limit that to looking between the differing sensibilities of the Latin-Western and the Greek-Eastern traditions of Hellenic thought. These views can be situated within the historical disputes of the Great Schism of 1054 that divided the Roman Catholic and Eastern Orthodox churches. In this overlap of institutional creed, culture, and language we also begin to see that philosophy does not have a monopoly over the genealogy of ontology—even today, in the "secular age" of modernity. Well beyond the terminology of the human person, the disputes between East and West are as deeply philosophical and political as they are religious and theological.

This may cause some discomfort to those who would like to sweep historical and ecclesial religious ideas under the rug of the "private," or those who see them as outdated, irrelevant, and dangerous. As dangerous as it might be to speak of religion in this historical way without apologies, there are two stark facts that make such an unapologetic risk reasonable. First, to sterilize an entire realm of experience and belief into an ahistorical domain is highly unlikely to ever succeed. We might go as far as to call it ontologically impossible. That alone bespeaks a tremendous impracticality. A secularization of this sort intuits as plausibly as the idea of censoring love or hate into this certain place and demanding emotional neutrality in another, wholly separate place. Second, there is a calculus to such a segregation that seems questionable. The dictum from Tacitus, "*Atque ubi colitudinum faciunt pacem apellat*" seems appropriate: in English, "They create desolation and call it peace."

To investigate the questions of the human person in the estuary of philosophy and theology, this mixed place of fresh and salted water, is not only reasonable. The desolate alternative reveals that it is also appropriate. Having made this defense of the integration of faith and reason for this investigation, I should also remark that my interests here are better described as philosophical anthropology or philosophical theology than as theology proper.

LATIN AND GREEK, "PERSON" AND PERSON

An etymological comparison, pure and simple, fails to convey the convergences and differences between the Latin "person" (a legal term) and the Greek
person (a radical thing). Under, over, and alongside the linguistic variations
are an array of historical and cultural preferences that offer insight into the
disputes of our day. (Especially those surrounding the questions of political liberalism, a question I will not take up here.) In other words, I do not
present them here for multicultural observation or comparison. They are not
equal to each other in my mind, but they do illuminate a serious conceptual
distinction, concealing a phenomenological reality. To begin with, one is terminological and the other is existential. There is also a certain defensiveness
about the Latin "person" of the West that, in my view, makes the Greek sense
of person more fertile, tragic, and phenomenologically honest. In many ways,
it is this very distinction between "person" and person that sets the battlefield
over it and its synonyms and antonyms. At their root, we find one of the
earliest and most basic divides in the *philosophia perennis*, the classic divide
of Hellenic thought: the general—and all too easily caricatured and oversim-
plified—difference between Plato and Aristotle.

In the West, ever since the integration of Aristotle into the philosophy
and theology of Thomas Aquinas, via the Arabic philosopher Averroes, we
find momentum building towards a particularly "Western" approach to life.
This, of course, culminates in the early-modern rejection of scholasticism
and enters into the political philosophies and practices of liberalism. What
we find beforehand, however, is that the legal system of the Roman Empire
and the theology of the Holy Roman Empire, mixed with the philosophy of
Aristotle, carry over a sense of personhood that remains with the West to
this day and culminates with the most radical human invention of all time:
the autonomous individual, now fading into the *homo economicus*. This
invention, and neoliberal progression, inaugurates what Foucault regards
to be "the death of man."[3]

The best source that I know of for this purpose is *Person and Being*
by the neo-Thomistic Jesuit, W. Norris Clarke. The book itself has Western
sensibilities. It is brief, systematic, and practical. However, too much can
be made and inferred from these generalities of "the West." To take them
too far would be a mistake. The book is also insightful, straightforward,

---

3. Foucault, *Order of Things*, 342.

and offers rich passages on, and analysis of, the person that exceeds the terminological "person."

Clarke describes the Western "person" as "a distinct entity beginning as a social and legal term in Roman law, where 'person' meant a human being with full legal rights as a Roman citizen, as distinguished from slaves, who were indeed human beings, but not persons." He moves from Roman law to the uses of the term "person" in early Christian theology as follows:

> But the most urgent pressure came from the Christian theologians to explicate more precisely the two central Christian doctrines of God as Triune (one God, with one divine nature possessed equally by three "owner" or persons) and the Incarnation (God become man in Jesus Christ, so that the human nature of Jesus is not a person on its own but is "owned" by the Second Divine Person, the Son, who now possess two natures, one divine, possessed from all eternity, the other human, taken on in time).[4]

Clarke sees this theological use of the term as a transition of the term "person" from the social or legal realm into the realm of theological trans-action. This marriage of the "person" of Rome and the "person" of Christian Trinitarian theology that begins to carve out a prototype, of the Western notion of personhood. Fusing the legal and the theological demands of the term, Clarke describes Aquinas's sense of personhood in the following way: "In a word, in perhaps the briefest—and still one of the best—descriptions of person ever given, a person is a being that is *dominus sui*, that is, master of itself, or *self-possessing* (in the order of knowledge by self-consciousness, in the order of will and action by self-determination and free will)."[5]

This description of "person" is striking in many ways. To begin with, it is nearly identical to what would later become the individual of modernity. It bears the mark of autonomy, even before the political system for this autonomous self to live in had been thought of. On this reading, Aquinas's person, harkening back to Rome, is as responsible for the modern self as Descartes's *cogito*. It would be a mistake, however, to think that Clarke or Aquinas had a superficial sense of personhood. The *dominus sui* is not the exact same thing as the autonomous, modern "individual." For Thomists, things grow according to nature. Faithful to this tradition, Clarke offers this rich insight into what he calls "an actualized person," i.e., a person who has been perfected according to nature: "To be an actualized person, then, is to

4. Clarke, *Person and Being*, 25.

5. Ibid., 25–26.

be a lover, to live a life of inter-personal self-giving and receiving. Person is essentially a 'we' term. Person exists in its fullness only in the plural."[6]

The question becomes, why? If the person is in fact a "we" term, then, why does Clarke remain faithful to Aquinas's *dominus sui*? The answer to that question is to be found in the introduction. Here, Clarke reveals his own motives and the overall defensive posture of the "person" of the West, leaning heavily on Aristotle's notion of substance:

> There is another more urgent reason for undertaking this "creative completion" today. The second part of our [20th] century has seen a rich development of the relational aspects of the person, worked out by existential phenomenologists and personalists of various schools, as well as by schools of psychology and psychotherapy, extending from Heidegger to Sartre, Gabriel Marcel, Emmanuel Mounier and the French personalists, Martin Buber, Levinas, John Macmurray, Viktor Frankl, and many others. St. Thomas himself would have been delighted, I think, with these rich phenomenological analyses of our time, since this aspect of his own thought was only very sketchily developed. Yet these valuable analyses have almost without exception been suspicious of, or entirely hostile towards the notion of person as *substance*, which was so heavily stressed in the classical tradition—ancient, medieval, and early modern. As a result, the being of the person has been explained so onesidedly in terms of relation and systems of relations that the dimension of the person as abiding self-identity, interiority, and in-itselfness has tended to disappear from sight, or at least lose all metaphysical grounding. Here we are faced, on the one hand, with a rich older metaphysical tradition of the person that has left the relational dimension underdeveloped and, on the other, with a more recent phenomenological tradition that has highly developed the relational aspect but lost its metaphysical grounding.[7]

This is Clarke's descriptive claim. His argument attempts to reconcile these two articulations of personhood and defend the view that all of it can be found in the vast resources of philosophical and theological Thomism. He claims that there is a metaphysical grounding to be had on the *inside*, so to speak, of the "person." This radical interiority is similar to what John Crosby describes, in *The Selfhood of the Human Person*, as "incommunicability." This is where Clarke is quintessentially Latin and Western: his belief that relationality is a mere aspect of the person, one among many. His

6. Clarke, *Person and Being*, 76.

7. Ibid., 4–5.

metaphysical approach favors the part from the whole because it is based in a disembodied metaphysics that separates—or needlessly expands—the person and the world into two distinct realities. That is why he seems to find the locality of interiority to serve as a metaphysical anchor for the term "person" and its referent, the existing human person.

We find a radically different approach in Christos Yannaras's magnificent work, *Person and Eros*.[8] In the ways that Clarke's book is Western, Yannaras's is strikingly Eastern. While Clarke's *Person and Being* is just over one hundred pages, Yannaras's *Person and Eros* is just shy of four hundred. While Clarke is clear, systematic, and fairly practical, Yannaras is dense, sporadic, and mystical. At the same time, Yannaras's sense of person begins with an etymology that extracts an ontological and existential reality. In other words, for Yannaras, the person is not primarily semantic or terminological, and the metaphysics of personhood, while they can be illuminated through language, flow from existence. Here, the precision and nuance— but most of all the antiquity—of the Greek language serve him well.

Yannaras wastes no time. He begins in this way:

> By the word *prospon* ("person") we define a referential reality. The referential character of the term is revealed fundamentally by its primitive use, that is, by its grammatical construction and etymology. The presupposition *pros* ("towards") together with the noun *ops* (*opos* in the genitive), which means "eye," "face," "countenance," form the composite word *pros-opon*: I have my face turned towards someone or something; I am opposite someone or something. The words thus functioned initially as a term indicating an immediate reference, a relationship. *Prospon*, or person, is defined as reference and relation and itself defines a reference and relation. The word's primordial semantic content does not allow us to interpret personhood simply as individuality outside the field of relation.

The clarity of this passage is remarkable. From the genetic "semantic content" of the term we find a path towards a metaphysics that is irreducible. The interiority of the person and the field of relations in which it exists are not points of disputation here, they simply are the case in complete totality. The whole human person for Yannaras, then, is *"all light, all face, all eye"* [emphasis mine]. Yannaras ends by completing his opening move in this passage:

8. I am deeply grateful to Gary Perkerwicz, who recommended the book to me in the most generous way possible: by purchasing it for me.

For the person to be restored to his or her integrity and wholeness, for the human being to become "all *prospon*"—"all person"—defines our existential end. It is the conclusion of our moral journey, the attainment of theosis or deification, the goal towards which our Church strives—as defined by Macarius of Egypt when he wrote: "For the soul that has been deemed worthy to participate in the spirit of his (God's) light and has been made radiant by the beauty of his ineffable glory, since he has prepared it for himself as a throne and dwelling-place, becomes all light, all face, all eye."[9]

This brings about a conclusion that escapes the Western sensibilities of Clarke. Namely, that *individuals do not exist*. Any form of personhood that denies this reality will only serve to alienate the person from herself. As Martin Buber—a Western thinker—put it in *I and Thou*: "In the beginning is the relation."[10]

This relational insight is not a transactional notion of relationship; it is irreducible. It does not require an external relation to complement or interrupt the always-already relational human person. This need not be mystical, however. We arrive, at birth, in relationship, covered in blood. In this sense, the human person is a public unto herself, from womb to tomb. Any community of human persons, then, is a multiplication by degrees of existential plurality, not a zero sum ontogenesis.

When we think of the notion of a "public school," that enrolls and socializes essentially private individuals, we realize that the result of the existential annihilation of the individual subverts the assumption that schools become necessary for public reasons. The situation is indeed far more radical: the human person already constitutes a public before entering the school or any other site of social relations. The point, then, of the public institution is not an exception to a private understanding of personhood. Furthermore, describing this site in terms of the human persons for whom privacy acts as a deprivation is a violent choice and an unnecessary one. After all, the teacher is there. She can offer not from a public institutional identity, but from her own human personhood that also begins as a public. For this reason, democratic and liberal notions that favor such institutions for their public identity do themselves serious harm in the process by reifying the assumption that ignores the human person as a public. This raises

9. Yannaras, *Person and Eros*, 293.

10. Buber, *I and Thou*, 69. It is also worth mentioning Buber's excellent essay on education that relates to many of these reflections in the collection of his essays, entitled *Between Man and Man*.

political questions, to be sure, but, more crucially for this study, it confirms the eros of study that through subsistence demands an embodied and amorous theory of human personhood.

TRAGIC LOVER

In *The Erotic Phenomenon*, Jean-Luc Marion remarks that, in the original Latin of Descartes's *Meditations*, the *ego* is described excluding love.[11] The first translator of Descartes from Latin into French, Duc de Luynes, added "which loves, which hates" to the opening of Descartes's Third Meditation.[12] Marion favors this revision—albeit a revision unintended by Descartes—and exhorts us to take up Duc de Luynes's addition to the *ego* and see ourselves "as the *cogitans* that thinks insofar as it first loves, in short as the lover (*ego amans*) . . . substituting for the *ego cogito*, which does not love."[13] This challenges the ontological implication of Descartes's *cogito* and affirms Augustine's claim: *Nemo est qui non amet—without love, I would be nothing*. In other words, I do not think and therefore I exist, as Descartes would have it; I love and therefore exist and think and love again (and again and again). The eros of study, dwelling within the desirous abyss of Being, confirm our embodied existence.

Marion's exhortation against Descartes's *cogito* also takes the form of a question and answer. He asks, "Why is love thrown to the wind, why is it refused an erotic rationality?" He replies to his own question, saying:

> The answer is not hidden far away: because love is defined as a passion, and therefore as a derivative modality, indeed as an option to the "subject" . . . And, in fact, we think of ourselves most

11. Marion, *Erotic Phenomenon*, 6–8. In Descartes, this description can be found in the first paragraph of Meditation Three, "Concerning God That He Exists." The original, 1641 Latin passage is: "Ego sum res cogitans, id est dubitans, affirmans, negans, pauca intelligens, multa ignorans, volens, nolens, imaginans etiam & sentiens . . ." All three versions are available for free online at: Descartes, *Meditations*, http://www.wright.edu/cola/descartes/intro.html.

12. The 1647 French translation is: "Je suis une chose qui pense, c'est-à-dire qui doute, qui affirme, qui nie, qui connaît peu de choses, qui en ignore beaucoup, qui aime, qui hait, qui veut, qui ne veut pas, qui imagine aussi, et qui sent." This translates into the 1901 English translation, by John Veltch, which retains Duc de Luynes's addition parenthetically. It reads as follows: "I am a thinking thing, that is, a being who doubts, affirms, denies, knows a few objects, and is ignorant of many, [*who loves, hates*], wills, refuses, who imagines likewise, and perceives . . ." (emphasis mine, enclosure in original); ibid.

13. Marion, *Erotic Phenomenon*, 8.

of the time as just such an ego, a being who cogitates orderable and measurable objects, so that we no longer look upon our erotic events except as incalculable and disordered accidents happily marginalized, indeed optional . . .[14]

Earlier in the book, Marion makes this striking statement:

> The result of these failed efforts is that ordinary people, or, put another way, all those who love without knowing what love wants to say, or what it wants of them, or above all how to survive it— that is to say, you and I first and foremost—believe themselves condemned to feed on scraps: desperate sentimentalism of popular prose, the frustrated pornography of the idol industry, or the shapeless ideology of that boastful asphyxiation known as "self-actualization." Thus philosophy keeps quiet, and in this silence love fades away.[15]

For Marion, this silence of philosophy is neither a disciplinary silence in academia nor a problem in the history of philosophy. It is, first and foremost, the silence of *philo-sophia*: love of wisdom. It is the alienated silence of love to itself, the restraining of eros from its passion fruit, love. This strange philosophical forgetting of love is even more prescient and fundamental to Marion than the neglect of Being noted by Heidegger in *Being and Time*, and it is also, perhaps, a more radical remembrance. This is because, for Marion, the very terms of our existence are at stake when the human person is mistaken for anything but a lover.

It may also be helpful to cite a similar view from Charles Taylor's book *A Secular Age* (published the same year, 2007, as the English publication of Marion's *Erotic Phenomenon*) via a fine review of the book written by Peter Gordon.[16] Like Foucault's genealogies—whose source is not power, pure and simple, but the production of the subject by biopower—so too, on Gordon's reading, is Taylor's *A Secular Age* described in terms of how its "disciplinary society" built a "new model of the human being."

> With the rise of the disciplinary society Taylor also sees a change in the very conception of human being. The older conception of the self as embedded in a holistic but differentiated

14. Marion, *Erotic Phenomenon*, 6.

15. Ibid., 2.

16. Gordon, "Place of the Sacred," 647–73. At the time I originally wrote this chapter I had not yet finished *A Secular Age*; now that I have finished it I find Gordon's review even more helpful and accurate.

natural-social-theological order slowly gave way to a "disembedded" selfhood understood to be ontologically prior to and independent of its surroundings. The realist conception of the world as the bearer of intrinsic meanings to which we must conform was supplanted by the notion that the only orders we must acknowledge are those we construct for ourselves. The social imaginary no longer envisioned as an interdependent system working in concert but a dispersal of atomistic individuals only to themselves and only contingently responsive to those around them.[17]

This new human person that Taylor sees as the hallmark of the disciplinary society built by the Secular Age—modernism, in other words—is strikingly similar to Descartes's *ego cogito* critiqued by Marion, and anticipated by Aquinas's *dominus sui*. Taylor calls it "the buffered self." This "buffered self" is the kind of self that, according to Taylor, replaced the "porous self" during the modern, secular Enlightenment. Gordon describes Taylor's "buffered self" as one that is "assertive, rationalistic and stakes a claim to autarky that shuts down its experience of intimacy even in relation to its own bodily passions."[18]

In striking similarity to the dialectic of Descartes's *ego cogito* vs. Duc de Luynes's *ego amans* we find in Marion, Taylor's description of the buffered and porous self brings out the tragic elements of the lover. These are elements that, for Taylor, come cloaked in religious mysticism:

> Living in a disenchanted world, the buffered self is no longer open, vulnerable to a world of spirits and forces which cross the boundary of the mind, indeed, negate the very idea of there being a secure boundary. The fears, anxieties, even terrors that belong to the porous self are behind it. This sense of self-possession, of a secure inner mental realm, is all stronger, if in addition to disenchanting the world, we have also taken the anthropocentric turn and no longer even draw upon the power of God.[19]

As I argued earlier, we cannot ignore Taylor's demand for a theological turn—a turn shared by recent French phenomenology (Levinas, Ricœur,

---

17. Ibid., 661–62.
18. Ibid., 662.
19. Ibid.

Marion, et al.)[20] and Slavoj Žižek's atheist "materialist theology,"[21] among many others. Yet, even if we pay the theological aspects little attention, the description of the dispossessed and insecure *porous self* as something fearful, anxious, and even terrorized adds a layer of tragic funk to the *ego amans* of Marion. This marriage of an amorous *ego* and a porous self is ultimately a matter of understanding, in that deep ontological sense of existential intimacy that to offer true love is to be a tragic lover: the lover who offers without expectation or assurance that the offering will actualize into a gift. This rejects the nihilist nonfortune of modern (neo)liberal individualism and allows the human person to again be thrown into the flux of relations in the world of Being, the subsistent life-world, embodied in an amorous and tragic existence, come what may.

Again: This is the human person who cannot be removed from the world of Being, nor deny the subsistent life-forces that act in complex ways to reveal the erotic proximity of existence. This is the whole human person, the one we hope to become through a love that cannot be given—only offered. This is what my son taught me when he became my teacher and ontologically asserted, "I am not a goose!"

WHO SHALL WE TEACH?—TEACHERS

When we see it in its barest form, the art of teaching is the art of existing, the art of becoming a human person, of growing and enriching the public and communal life of the human person who annihilates the individual without sacrificing herself at the altar of a plastic and technocratic public. To teach requires a relational ontology that might seem to overlap the already present ontology of the human person. But here is the answer to our riddle: *there is no ontological distinction between the existential reality of the human person and the teacher.* Because of this, the task of teaching can be found in the communal demands of existence, within the complete fabric of the world, animated by the eros of study. This suggests the fundamental import of ontology and phenomenology for teaching. It also points to the tragic form of love that teaching requires. Love of flesh and bones. Facing

---

20. See the (translated) 1991 report by Dominique Janicaud (with replies from several scholars mentioned in the report, including Marion and Ricœur), *Phenomenology and the "Theological Turn."*

21. See Žižek's most recent book *The Monstrosity of Christ*, written along with John Milbank, and Žižek's earlier works: *The Fragile Absolute* and *The Puppet and the Dwarf.*

these ontological requisites, the question becomes "Who?"—*Who shall we teach?*

Leaving aside the broad cultural and political replies one might present to this question, we can imagine the process of entering the classroom—wherever that may be—to encounter the student. Who will it be? A mystery? A ghost? Or perhaps a human person: that singular embodiment that is ontologically plural. The broad and general critique of the times tells us that human persons are something of an endangered species, and this is mostly true. But when a teacher encounters a student, we find a moment that is new and pregnant with imagination for the human person to reappear as a tragic lover, possessed by the eros of study and the irreducible posture of the teacher. Thus, these pages are not for the dreamer, they are for the teacher. Education, then, becomes a site of hope for tragic transformation for those who dwell in it and suffer its fortune and existential reality.

To be specific, I am thinking of the actual, physical, mental, and spiritual approach—the phenomenological event. The memory that today is the first day to teach; gathering of books, syllabi, class roster, and/or other teaching things into a stack or putting them into a bag or box; walking down the hall while adjusting a waistline, necktie, or collar, wondering where the room is; running a hand through the hair or checking the make-up; stopping to use the bathroom or get a drink of water, all the while wondering: Who will I find inside that room? What room is it again? How many will come to meet me? Who will those names on the roster become in the flesh? How will they appear to me? What will they look like? Do I have eyes for them? What will they disclose and what will remain hidden? Who will I see? Will they like me? Shall I love them? Would they even care? Will we live or die?

Those curiosities before one enters a classroom for the first time are not so different from the "first-day-of-school" feelings a student also has on this day too, especially if they do not know the teacher or the class beforehand. This particular event is not limited to the schoolhouse, but that does seem to be a widely available and poignant time and place to begin things anew, to put the human person into the ancient relations of tragic love. To face the question "Who shall we teach?" is to offer the response "Human persons we find in existence."

The demands of this question are very specific. The existential question of teaching is the question of "who." The other questions we might ask—what, where, or how—are ordered by this question. This order reveals another paradox: the "what" question of Being cannot be answered without the question of "who" that brings it into existence through the life forces of subsistence. When we ask that question again and again, we face both the perennial challenge to exist as a human person and the current crisis of disenchanted individualism, the sterilization of the public through the political fiction of the private. The point is not to reorder the private; the point is to reject it as an ontological impostor. We must struggle for love against nihilism.

After the image of the human person tragic lover is seen, then, the question reappears: Who shall we teach? This time, the answer slowly becomes slightly different: Who is teaching? Who is the teacher? It is fashionable to blur the line between teacher and student. Ontologically speaking, this would be overly complicated. The simple fact is that persons are teachers, moved by erotic study, living amidst the mystery of education that we find ourselves in.

This is our task: to be, live, and exist by seeking Being, sensing subsistence, and seeing existence. In short, to teach by offering ourselves as we are, without expectation or despair, filled with fragile hope.

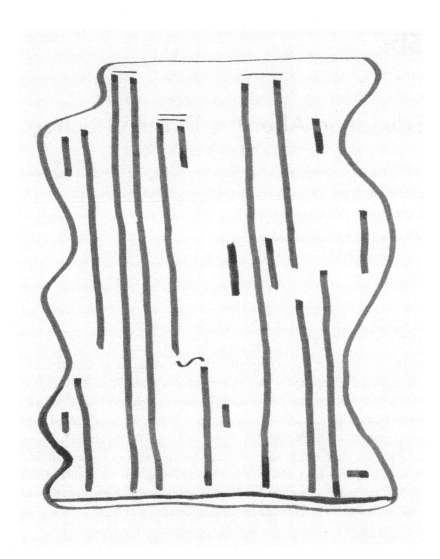

Six

Education After the Death of School

For my own part, then, so far as logic goes, I am willing that every leaf that ever grew in this world's forests and rustled in the breeze should become immortal. It is purely a question of fact: are the leaves so, or not?

WILLIAM JAMES, *HUMAN IMMORTALITY*

QUESTIONS

At the end of these chapters, pertinent questions remain. There are understandable reasons to be skeptical about this work. To begin with, the results of the descriptions offered in the previous chapters have not narrowly focused on education, study, and the person, but have instead tried to imagine those sites of reality through a looking glass, the trinitarian lens. In doing so, these things have not been brought into clear view. In fact, these descriptions have tried to focus by expansion—by zooming out, not in. This expanded vision has been chosen over clearer, narrower views in order to remain faithful to the ontological breadth and depth of things. In doing so, however, our sight is likely to appear darker and less clear.

A few things can be clarified. (1) Education has been described as something ontological in the most radical sense, distinct from the politics of schooling and the psychology of teaching. (2) A contextual theory of education proposes an ontological and foundational theory of education that can support not only the presence of schooling, but also study, and

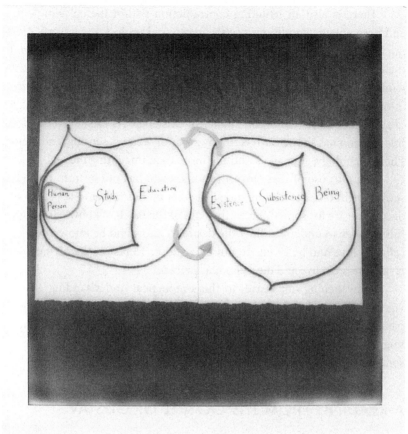

teaching. (2) Study has been presented as an intermediary erotic force, largely outside our immediate will and voluntary attention. (3) Teaching becomes the existential recovery of the human person as a public and the offering emerges, requiring no transaction or just deserts. Together these strands of ideas, and the trinitarian lens used to describe them, reveal their internal order and amount to the beginning development of what may become folk phenomenology. In future work to come I hope to show, in various ways, what this "folkloric reversal" is, and how it distinguishes itself and makes space for a phenomenology rooted in art, in what can only be shown and offered.

There is also an irritating contradiction within the epistemological and hermeneutic conditions of this ontological project, the poverty of using language to describe the ineffable—to *say* what can only be *shown*. In the end, it might be disheartening or even maddening to realize that the trinitarian lens is not a prescriptive technology, but instead, a way of imagining things with fidelity to the context of Being, the forces and energies of subsistence, and the bodily matter of existence. As each exercise of the imagination has shown us: it is simply a way of seeking, sensing, and seeing. Phenomenology, after all, is nothing more than imagining the real.

The purpose of these investigations, then, has not been to make descriptions in order to obtain knowledge-about, but rather to appeal to our deepest desire for something entirely out of the reach of knowledge, something closer to understanding: the desire to know and be known *ontologically*. To love and be loved. To not be a goose. To rest in the divine sea of restlessness. To live and die as human persons.

Reawakening our senses to this ontological understanding also invigorates our awareness of the lasting potentiality hidden in the ontological passions. This "invigoration" is what re-enchantment is—to show that what might have appeared to be dead is alive, to vindicate the fruitfulness of something against the barrenness of nothing.

A READING FROM THE GOSPEL OF GUSTAV

(Kafka) "The hangman is today a respectable bureaucrat, relatively high up on the civil service payroll. Why shouldn't there be a hangman concealed in every conscientious bureaucrat?"

(Janouch) "But bureaucrats don't hang anybody!"

(Kafka) "Oh don't they!" . . . "They transform human beings into dead code numbers, incapable of any change."[1]

COCKROACHES AND HEIRLOOM TOMATOES

A sterile species is in constant crisis. A fertile species has its trials, but, at the very least, it is ontologically sustainable. It *is* and can *be*. Think, for instance, of the relative immortality and durability of the cockroach when

---

1. Janouch, *Conversations with Kafka.*

compared to the inverse qualities of the panda. Or, consider this difference between industrial and heirloom tomatoes: the seeds of *heirloom* tomatoes can be fruitfully planted, while *industrial* seeds cannot. Industrial agriculture only grows a few of the same strands of plants that have been domesticated by agroscience in order to be to be mass-produced, but not reproduced. The zenith of industrial fruit is seedless. Heirloom tomatoes are different: they are untamed, wild things that can sow their pregnant seed if given the chance, if they don't rot or get infested with bugs first. Unlike their domesticated cousins, heirloom tomatoes are capable of bearing fruit, for better and for worse. They are virile and fecund.

Following this basic distinction between cockroaches and heirloom tomatoes, on the one hand, and pandas and industrial tomatoes, on the other, one way to identify things is to see how virile and fertile they are; that is to say, whether or not they display potentiality verging on immortality. According to these criteria, we could speculate whether "education" is more like a cockroach and less like a panda, more like a fecund heirloom tomato and less like a neutered industrial one. Is our notion of "education" wild and fertile enough to endure and exceed the endangered and domesticated era we live in?

THE DEATH OF SCHOOL

These kinds of questions are not new. They are implied within the many "deaths" of the previous, murderous century: the death of God (via Nietzsche), the death of Man (via Foucault), the death of the Author (via Barthes), and more. Considering these "deaths," we might see them as a search for immortality: the potential for some live-thing to replace the dead-thing and prove to be more fertile and potent than its dead predecessor.

Let us consider another "death": *the death of school*. This would not be the abolition of schools or schooling. This would not be "deschooling," "unschooling," or any other historical end to state-sponsored compulsory schooling as the libertarians and anarchists suggest from time to time. Neither would "the death of school" be an axiomatic expression for those displeased with schooling these days, as Diane Ravitch tells us in *The Death and Life of the Great American School System*. No. As with the deaths of God, Man, and the Author, that do not imply that such things are descriptively extinct, but rather that they have been replaced by the hermeneutics of a different genealogy—so too with the death of school: the death of school would be a time when schools would continue to exist, but would cease to be believed in. The death of school would be a time of disenchantment when, like church attendance or book reading, people continue to attend and purchase, but know better than to believe in the idol as they once might have. They would ritually bring it food and drink, knowing all along that the statue cannot and does not ingest anything.

In dead schools, people would still come, as is the ordinary custom, but once they are there they would seek relief in anything that feels like an escape from the imposing deadness of the school. Like the office-worker who waits for an end to the torture of another day of sitting at her cubicle, surrounded by absurdity, trying to invent new ways to make time pass as painlessly as possible, so too with the dead school: the death of school would be when, like the Gods and Kings of yesteryear, the school is exposed as a fraud, but the alternatives seem even more terrifying, so nothing is done. We agree to die before death itself for fear of the cost of living. The death of school is when the stupidity of things sets in, and Sartrean *nausea* ensues, but we sit in our pews, cubicles, or desks anyway. When, like Kafka, we faithfully go to work for the "hangman."

Perhaps the school is dying or is dead already. And, perhaps, it is not. A telling sign might be when teachers hate to be students—and, consequently, hate to be teachers—yet are equally committed to making their own students be and do that which they themselves hate. Whether this is ever the case today or not, the death of school presents a useful litmus test for studying the metaphysics of education. Could this thing called "education" withstand the death of school? If the school were to pass away, would we find any fruit born from this mysterious thing called "education," or would we encounter a neutered shell leftover from a sterile, domesticated fruit? Furthermore, if the school *is* dying, or is dead already, could this thing called "education" offer any relief to you and me, amidst this existential malaise of stupidity and deadness?

This line of questioning is not new. It is ancient. We can find it expressed by the "Parable of the Sower" in the synoptic gospels, or in Plato's *Phaedrus*, where Socrates asks (and replies):

> Would a husbandman, who is a man of sense, take the seeds, which he values and which he wishes to bear fruit, and in sober seriousness plant them during the heat of summer, in some garden of Adonis, that he may rejoice when he sees them in eight days

appearing in beauty? At least he would do so, if at all, only for the sake of amusement and pastime.[2]

There may be industrialized fruit born from conceptions of education that emerge from the narrow womb of the politics of modern-day compulsory schooling and the psychometrics of managerial teaching, but when that neutered fruit dies, what will replace it? Furthermore, as Jesus and Socrates tell us: these "sowers" cannot be sober or serious about what they are doing. Perhaps they are amusing themselves, just playing around, or putting in a good day's work for the hangman. Who knows?

As we have seen, my own orientation to the philosophy of education makes a sharp distinction between forms of educational research that claim to be concerned with education (but are often disinterested in it, looking for ways to replicate children into Kafka's hangman) on the one hand, and educational research that is serious about what "education" might be in and out of schools on the other. In other words, "education after the death of school" provides a pragmatic metaphysics for attempting to decipher between the chaff and the grain of pedagogic literature.

Philosophy of education is often misunderstood because education is confused with schooling, but make no mistake: it cannot ignore issues raised by the school; compulsory schools are rich places to consider philosophical questions about education. However, exclusive and narrow conceptions of education not only distort education, they libel and devalue teachers and create a bureaucratic class of anti-teachers, blind and ignorant of the nooses concealed within their policies and curricula.

Philosophy of education, insofar as it is serious, cannot separate these things. It cannot abandon the contemporary site of the school and its students and teachers, nor can it allow this political site to monopolize or domesticate the imagination of what education and teaching really are—which is not primarily epistemological, behavioral, or developmental; it is ontological, which is merely to say that it is real. We might ask ourselves, as a speculative exercise, how many papers and books would survive in the field of philosophy of education after the death of school?

I will not attempt to answer these questions myself. Instead, I will tell you a true story.

---

2. Plato, *Phaedrus.*

DRIVING TOMAS

I must admit: I have not frequently had the visions I have written about here. They are mostly hazy and dreamlike to me. In many ways, these words are written for myself in order to remember and be faithful to them. Here is a story of one time that I may have had something like a trinitarian vision.

The first time I drove with my newborn son, Tomas, my sight was ontologically changed. (My life was changed, too.) As I drove, I felt myself overwhelmed by the context of Being (Tomas being so new in the world, what was once nothing was now something, and more); I sensed the forces and energies and fortune of subsistence all around us as I watched my speedometer tell me that we were traveling at over fifty miles per hour and hoped his body was working well. Filled with emotion, I saw him existentially, in the flesh, in my rear-view mirror that reflected the "baby-mirror" that we installed in order to see him in his back-facing car seat, but I also saw him as my son, *Tomas Mateo Rocha*, someone I love and hope I would die for.

I saw all of this and more. It made me realize the frightening seriousness of this mundane thing I often do called "driving." It also made me well up with joy and love because of the beauty of driving in this particular way: as a lover, not an individual—as a father. I was painfully aware of the technology being used to travel at speeds that our bodies were not made to withstand—that could end in death. I was also intimately aware of the new life that joined me and re-enchanted my life. All at once, the sight of the existence of my son made me sense the subsistence I had previously been numb to, and this sensibility drew me to further seek Being and realize that, in fact, it was Being who first sought me. I did not "think" these things then. I lived them. Recalling them now, I desire to live them again. To be, subsist, and exist. To seek, sense, and see. In the moment, I offered a prayer of thanksgiving.

This is but a mangled picture of a real moment, and it cannot replace or recreate it. But this vision I had while driving my newborn son changed me. I have witnessed the same sort of thing various other times when I encountered the fragile and overwhelming reality of the personal existence of him, his brother, and his sister. Each time, it shows me a trinitarian vision that is mysterious, fortunate, erotic, and tragic. What I saw on that day was (and is still) beautiful, which made it real. These trinitarian visions I witnessed are the closest I have come to formulating a positive reply to my son's later objection, "I am not a goose!" A few years later, when he objected on his own behalf, he taught me to remember those transformative, trinitarian visions and summoned me to be faithful to them. I must now attempt, fail, and continue to show this fidelity through restlessness. Through love.

This story explains why I wrote this book and what it is for.

CONCLUSION: A DAY AT THE ZOO

I never intended to provide solutions to any problems. Instead, I hope to have offered an alternative to a problem-solving approach by doing what I have called "folk phenomenology": a theoretical, intuitive practice that might allow us to be, subsist, and exist through seeking, sensing, and seeing, resulting in a series of imperfect descriptions. I will conclude with one final story.

I went to the zoo. In the outdoor space where the gorillas usually play during the warm months, I saw a young woman. There were no gorillas in sight and she was just sitting there in the shade, under the tree house made for the gorillas to climb and sit on. I wondered who this person was and why she was just sitting there. She was dressed like a nurse. Perhaps she was a veterinarian of some kind. Wasn't there work for her to do? Was she on her break and had nowhere else to go? Was she some kind of mystic or a crazy person? Was I going crazy?

As I looked with more care, I saw that she had a tiny, newborn gorilla in her lap. It crawled into view and was trying to take her walkie-talkie. I came to find out that this baby was an orphan that the zoo had rescued. In order to provide for an orphaned baby gorilla, a person has to be with the baby the entire day. Not only do the zookeepers have to feed, bathe, play with, and protect the baby, *they have to be with it.* They have to just sit there, doing nothing—they have to *be-with.* The baby doesn't need to be fixed because it has not been made into a problem, even as an orphan. The baby just needs love through presence. This means that it needs to be-with others, to know that there is someone present, offering.

Human babies—and other babies, too—know how to be-with people. Many times they know this better than adults who have grown accustomed to alienation. They might know very little *about* this, but they know how to be-with someone. They certainly know when they are left alone—they protest loudly. My youngest daughter, Sofia, desires for me to hold her. She needs to be held. She does not want to be in my generic presence, she wants to be held and embraced. She reaches up and calls out in noises that have no semantic meaning but speak to me all the same. When she is content she will sigh or be silent.

Perhaps using this trinitarian lens will show us that we—human persons and the world in general—need exactly what this baby gorilla and human need: love, ontological—as opposed to purely sociological—community. Could this be education? *Seeking* Being, *sensing* subsistence, and *seeing* existence? Being, subsisting, and existing? Living in love and communion? I believe that it is one worthwhile place to start and perhaps even to finish, and to do this we cannot give anything. We can only offer because *everything that shows, offers.*

Without a constant renewal of this search for love and *theosis*, we are already orphaned to the emptiness of nihilism. But there is no need to be afraid, insofar as we can do and be otherwise. This final choice, to reject fear and embrace the courage to offer, is a new beginning and a beautiful end.

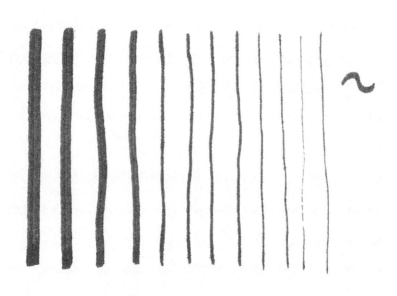

Afterword

by Eduardo M. Duarte

...the *actual* world! the *common sense! Contact! Contact! Who* are we? *Where* are we?

<small>HENRY DAVID THOREAU, *THE MAINE WOODS*[1]</small>

"I WAS NOT BORN to be forced. I will breathe after my own fashion."[2] The force here is meant to describe or denote an external power, a force from outside . . . Thoreau. But this force can*not* be Grace or Geist, Spirit, or *Espiritu*. It is another force, outside Thoreau, but not outside the human condition. Already we encounter a normative claim: an external force, let's call it the law, is violent insofar as it moves us against ourselves. We call this external force "the law" (*la ley*) in order to clarify it as a power constituted and instituted by humans to control, direct, and decide the actions of other humans. By contrast, the Divine Law and Nature's Law, which Aristotle identifies as the most powerful force,[3] are pre and post, before and beyond

---

1. Thoreau, "Ktaadn," 95.

2. Thoreau, "Civil Disobedience," 13.

3. Here is the important citation from Aristotle, *Rhetoric* (bk. 1, ch. 13): "By two kinds of law I mean particular law and universal law. Particular law is that which each community lays down and applies to its own members: this is partly written and partly unwritten. Universal law is the law of nature. For there really is, as every one to some extent divines, a natural justice and injustice that is binding on all men, even on those who have no association or covenant with each other. It is this that Sophocles's Antigone clearly means when she says that the burial of Polyneices was a just act in spite of the prohibition: she means that it was just by nature: 'Not of to-day or yesterday it is, / But lives eternal: none can date its birth'" (Sophocles, *Antigone*, 456–57).

the human; always already existing, and thus, from a human perspective, *eternal*. In this sense we are born *into* the Divine and Natural Law. "I was not born to be forced" can only refer to the human law (*la ley*). Thoreau's birth was *already* forced by the Divine and Natural laws. "To be" (*Being*), in this case, refers to a future that is happening: Being *qua* becoming. "To be forced" recalls the originary laws of becoming, the fundamental onto-logical force of natality: ceaseless nativity. "I was not born to be forced" is thus rather: "I was born to be." "To be forced" indicates the present future (Being *qua* becoming) into which Thoreau was born: ceaseless nativity. No human law can supersede the originary force of becoming that beckons the original existential and ontological question: "*Where* are we? *Who* are we?" To recall this originary force is to respond to the call of the original ques-tions. And this recollection is what is happening with the *folkoric reversal* via *folk phenomenology*.

Epochē ["reduction"]:

> *I take no position with respect to the world as existing* . . . of course, I, as an empirical and concrete subject, continue to participate in the natural attitude toward the world . . . but I make no use of it. It is suspended, put out of play, out of circulation, between parenthe-ses; and by this "reduction" . . . the surrounding world is no longer simply existing, but "phenomena of being."[4]

There are at least two dangers I am confronting as I begin to write this afterword to Rocha's *Folk Phenomenology*. The first is the one that Adorno identifies during his lecture course on Kant. [Incidentally, but not at all arbitrarily, Adorno is the one who prompted me to begin this afterword by identifying philosophical "dangers." These "perils" of philosophy—as opposed to the "pearls" that Arendt urges us to collect by diving into the deep waters of philosophy's history[5]—strike me as both a signpost that returns us to the Homeric roots of folk phenomenology (i.e., the trials and triumphs in *The Odyssey*), but also a symptomatic sign of the particular kind of neurosis afflicting modern philosophy that is acutely manifest in Descartes's *Meditations*, i.e., the signature skepticism of παρανοια (*para-noia*): at the onset, before any *thinking* can happen, we are compelled to identify any and all actual (not potential) dangers, and thereby avoid them at all costs. As it turns out, these two signs of philosophical danger (the

---

4. Lyotard, *Phenomenology*, 47.
5. Arendt, "Thinking," 212.

Homeric and Cartesian) constitute the two sides of Rocha's method: *folk phenomenology*.]

The first danger, which Adorno identifies, is the *thema probandum*. As Adorno describes it, this danger is, like all good traps, hidden. But what makes this trap especially dangerous is that it is hidden within reason itself. Something other than παρανοια, but equally capable of probing reason while remaining apart from reason, is required to avoid this trap. *Memory*, the original *reconnaissance*, is called up to recall what must be avoided at the onset of any philosophical meditation: the danger that forecloses upon spontaneity. We might call spontaneity the actualization of reason, which Adorno, following Kant, reminds us, has "a particular kind of intention." When we encounter the intentionality of reason, and, what's more, immerse ourselves within it, we are taken in by the destiny (movement) of thinking: "its secret design to achieve freedom or the fulfillment of the destiny of humankind."[6]

The danger of the *thema probandum* appears here for me as the lurking danger that "my words," here, appearing as they are *after* Rocha's, are already predetermined *by* Rocha's words. At all costs I must avoid the danger that my words "may in reality have been determined in advance, in the sense that you know in advance how it will end, what will emerge, and indeed what ought to emerge. In general, this takes the form of justifying something already known and existing." Adorno continues: "It may even be the case that certain modern philosophical trends, phenomenology for example, have come into being in response to this demand to follow the logic of the matter in hand and to abstain from any *thema probandum*."[7] My strategy here—and it must be a strategy because I apply not a method in this *post scriptum*—is to recognize what Adorno has said about phenomenology by affirming Rocha's project as a case in point. And to do this I must take up the fundamental stance of phenomenology that Husserl categorized as *epochē*, and thereby return to the beginning of Rocha's book, and to the fundamental claim: "art precedes metaphysics."

An "afterword" is an επιλογος: a λογος (word, truth) offered επι (in addition). And not unlike a eulogy (ευλογία), an afterword is a kind of blessing (*benediction*). The additional word must be spoken well (*benedicere*), and in this case the blessing is an affirmation of the folkloric reversal as a recollection, a memory of the original or fundamental claim: "art precedes metaphysics."

6. Adorno, *Kant's Critique of Pure Reason*, 58.

7. Ibid., 60–61.

I want to return to Rocha's single claim "art precedes metaphysics," by bracketing (*epochē*) all that comes after that claim, and most of what comes before it. What I want to include in what comes before is Rocha's mantra-like assertion that distinguishes between philosophy and philosophers.[8] And I want to collapse that distinction: philosophers do philosophy, and philosophers are taken up by students of philosophy, by those who are undertaking an apprenticeship in philosophy. It is a peculiar apprenticeship because it is ongoing: one *never* becomes a "master" of philosophy. One is, rather, *mastered* by philosophy. This is the peculiar wisdom (σοφια) of Socrates that humbly points beyond. Before Socrates, Heraclitus issued the protocol of all who take up philosophy via philosophers: to learn thinking, listen not to the sage, but to the Word (Λογος). Of course, the paradox or irony is that in order to hear the Word, we must first listen to the sage. The apprenticeship of philosophy begins with hearing philosophers. And thus the first question that arises in the wake of the return via the folkloric reversal to Rocha's claim "art precedes metaphysics" is: "Where do we find the philosophers *qua* artists, the artists qua philosophers?" (Hint from the young Nietzsche: anticipate the (re)birth of tragedy and listen for music-making philosophers.)

There is a genealogy at work with the folkloric reversal: historical, cultural, political, first; ontological and existential, second, which is to say, in a still more originary location. For example, we read the documented lecture of Adorno, and we remember his working with his students on Kant, and suddenly we are sitting in the early morning of 18th century Königsberg listening to Professor Kant lecturing, and through his voice we are taken directly to an encounter with the sublime improvisational move-ment of reasoning. The same might happen if we happen to be taken back to October 1961 via Impulse! Records to the Village Vanguard, where we encounter Coltrane, and listen to him performing live. Coltrane too will take us directly to an encounter with the sublime improvisational move-ment of free thinking, a.k.a. reasoning. Philosophers make philosophy and this work appears in the world, documented, recorded and thus alive for us to remember, to hear, and, through such listening, learn thinking.

"Art precedes metaphysics." Philosophers make philosophy. To make something via thinking is to make art. This is how Aristotle distinguished

8. *Folk Phenomenology*, 8–9. Rocha's philosophers v. philosophy distinction is put to work in Rocha's *Primer for Philosophy and Education*, which is the important prelude to the larger work, both in the sense of preceding it and preparing the way for it. In this sense, it is presumed the reader of *Folk Phenomenology* has read the *Primer*.

art from metaphysics: the desire to make versus the desire to understand. Thinking (art) *before* knowing (science).

In what sense does "art precede metaphysics" in the order of things? Is this a philosophical question or a philosopher's question? It is both and neither.

"Art precedes metaphysics." I return to this single claim because it calls my attention. Phenomenological bracketing (*epochē*) is not a method that we can deploy, a tool that is ready-to-hand. Rather, it is forced upon us by what claims our attention, our singular undivided attention. *Epochē* happens to us through that which is singular, and in that singularity is compelling. (*N.B.*: all so-called "ethics," specifically the "relational" kind, is only ever an anthropocentric rendering of the ontological event of *epochē*. In this sense "ethics" is a form of *la ley*, an application of human law.) "Art precedes metaphysics" calls us to what is made *before* the making of the law: the singular work of art as a mimetic re-presentation of the birth of the human person, a rebirth of the human person. Art is not simply renewal but baptismal: regenerating of the originary force. Through art we arise and stand *before* the law. Art offers what is not yet normalized, adjudicated, judged. Before we can know *what* a thing is, we only know *that* it is. "Art precedes metaphysics."

I want to respond to the call of this fundamental claim by taking it up as a fundamental claim *about* phenomenology, which is to say, as a fundamental claim about how fundamental claims work via phenomenology. Metaphysics *arrives* at fundamental claims. Phenomenology is the documentation of being claimed fundamentally. To be *claimed* is to be compelled, forced, moved. This is the way fundamental claims work via phenomenology. Aristotle, arguably the founder of phenomenology, categorized this claiming as the arrival of first principles via *intuition* (νοῦς). Through Aristotle we can return to the question, "In what sense does art precede metaphysics in the order of things?" and respond: in the sense that art is our first response to the offering of Being. Art proceeds from intuition of first principles.

"Art precedes metaphysics" is a fundamental claim about the order of things and our response to them. Art is our first response in the sense that making precedes knowing. Art is the work that documents spontaneity, the free movement of reasoning, the coming-into-being, becoming; life re-presented via human hands and hearts. And here is where we encounter the source of the force manifested through the birth of the human person, the rebirth of the human being as a some*one* and not simply a some*thing*, a who versus a what. The source of the force that moves us to make art is love. To say "force" is to enlist Aristotle's category of ενεργεια (energeia), or movement-of-spirit. Fergusson's translation is most helpful in this context, because the folkloric reversal is a movement-of-spirit, specifically, the movement of the gathering spirit (κοινονια) that enlists our attention.[9] The singular is compelling in its singularity, in the manner in which it appears before us uniquely, standing out and calling, demanding our attention.

The folkloric reversal is the rehearsal of that original demand, the retrieval of the originary stance of phenomenology (*epoché*). What is this "originary stance"? First, it is originary in the sense of being first in the reception of Being. That is, it is an originary stance that stands with art. The originary stance of phenomenology receives the arrival of that which arrives first. Thus the folkloric reversal is a return to the appearance of the world as an ongoing offering (ceaseless nativity).[10] Being is offered, and that art is not simply our response to that offering, but our taking up of the offering *as* an offering, as the ongoing arrival of Being. Art emerges from our entering into that flow of becoming and mimetically re-presenting the experience of that flow. Phenomenology: the truth (λογος) of that which appears (φαίνομαι).[11]

The folkloric reversal, the movement into folk phenomenology, the retrieval of the originary stance, is the movement-of-spirit back to the original response to the originary offering. Folk phenomenology is a return to art. And if art is the original response to the originary offering of Being, then folk phenomenology is a proper recollection of Being. We *re-member* Being when we take up folk phenomenology, which, existentially, entails the manifestation of our own coming-into-being, the actualization of our singularity. This is the moment the young Nietzsche described as "the artist as artwork, the individual human subject as subjected to the totality of Being, the Primal Unity."[12] What is entailed with the reversal is a return, which we can describe as the Eternal Recurrence of Being happening via the subject, the thinker qua artist. "He is no longer an artist, he has become

---

9. Francis Fergusson, introduction to *Poetics*, by Aristotle, trans. Butcher.

10. Duarte, *Being and Learning*.

11. For an alternative etymological hermeneutic unpacking of "phenomenology," see Heidegger's "Clarification of the Name 'Phenomenology,'" sect. 9 of *History of the Concept of Time*.

12. Nietzsche, *Birth of Tragedy*, 4.

a work of art."[13] This is an event of production. To reduce it to "description" is to render this dramatic working out of the original a deprived form of metaphysics; a project deprived of its actuality, reduced to potency that forecloses upon action, so that what we are left with is impotency.

> First of all, however, we must conceive the folk-song as the musical mirror of the world, as the *original* melody . . .[14]

"Art precedes metaphysics." The folkloric reversal is a return to production and, in this sense of reversal of the degenerative reduction of phenomenology, to facile description. The reversal is thus a call to return to the ground of poetics, to the originary response of art as ποιέω: to bring about, make, render. This is fabrication, creation, production, but also the desire to undertake. The reversal returns us to the priority of being-made and thus of making. The artist becomes the work of art in music-making philosophy, folk phenomenology. This is learning as the re-collection of Being's offering, the working-out of subjectivity as singularity. In this sense, folk phenomenology is a return that propels a new forward movement. The young Heidegger described the temporality of this sort of movement as running ahead to the past.[15] With the making of art we have the possibility of realizing this double-movement that simultaneously leaps ahead by returning to the ground. With art we leap *into* the *Urgrund* (primal ground). In this sense the return to the "folk" is a return to our "roots." The folkloric reversal is a return to the making that happens before we do theory. And this is an important distinction. "Art precedes metaphysics" identifies that ποιέω precedes επίστεμε. In the Aristotelian catalogue we have three movements of spirit: the movement of making (τέχνη), the movement of acting (πραχις), and the movement of understanding (επίστεμε). The questions that resound, here, at the end, are: How will the *beyond* of the foregoing prolegomenon offered by Rocha, that announces the folkloric reversal, with the phenomenological work moving forward, in fact return to what precedes metaphysics? How will it leap ahead back to art? How will phenomenology *become* the work of folk, music-making philosophy, folk music? And who will hear and convey the *original* melody?

13. Ibid.

14. Ibid., 17 (emphasis mine).

15. Heidegger, *Concept of Time*. Heidegger writes: "This past, as that to which I run ahead, here makes a discovery in my running ahead to it: it is *my* past . . . This past is not a 'what,' but a 'how,' indeed the authentic 'how' of my Dasein . . . Running ahead to the past is Dasein's running up against its most extreme possibility."

Acknowledgments

THIS BOOK WAS FIRST drafted at the Ohio State University in Columbus, Ohio, during the late summer and early fall of 2009. It has been heavily edited and revised over a period of six years, benefitting from advice, encouragement, and generous criticism from many colleagues and friends. I owe them all a great debt of gratitude but first I thank my wife, Anne, and my family who have endured so much for the sake of my work and have inspired all of it. I also thank my doctoral advisor, Phil Smith, and co-advisor, Bryan Warnick, and the members of my doctoral committee: Timothy Leonard, Bill Taylor (may he rest in peace), and Patti Lather; I thank friends who read various versions and drafts, providing me feedback and support along the way: Ryan Thursday Adams, Vanessa Andreotti, Rene Arcilla, David Backer, Deborah Butler, Gert Biesta, Walter Gershon, Jessica Hochman, Tyson Lewis, Jennifer Logue, Silas Morgan, Paul Myhre, Michael Peters, Troy Richardson, Claudia Ruitenberg, Doris Santoro, and Stephen Webb; I thank those who have read and used drafts of the book in their own work, helping me to understand it better: Dan Clegg, Brad Rowe, Les Sabiston, Derek Tannis, and Justin Tse; I thank my students at Wabash College who endured reading it during my fall 2011 philosophy of education class; I thank my editors, Kaya Oakes and Artur Rosman, and my copyeditors Robert Dixon and Joseph and Natalie Antoniello, my photographer, Mike Blaha, my research assistant, Sarah McCabe, and the skilled team at Wipf and Stock, especially Christian Amondson; and I especially thank the two mentors who contributed directly to these pages in the foreword and afterword: Bill Pinar and Eduardo Duarte—a million thanks to everyone. All errors and mistakes are my own.

Credits

This work first appeared as my doctoral dissertation, *Education, Study, and the Person*, defended in 2010, which was awarded one of the Loadman Dissertation Prizes in the department of Educational Leadership and Policy at the Ohio State University School of Education and Human Ecology. Some of the content in several chapters has appeared in four adapted and modified articles I published between 2009 and this writing. They are as follows: From chapter one, "Educación de Carne y Hueso, Education of Flesh and Bone: Variations on a Folk Melody," published in *Lapíz* No. 1, 2014. From chapters two and three: "Education as Mystery: The Enchanting Hope of Desire," published in *Educational Philosophy and Theory*, 2015. From chapter four: "Erotic Study: Fortune, Baby-Talk, and Jazz" published in *Philosophy of Education*, 2012. And finally, from chapter five: "A Return to Love in William James and Jean-Luc Marion," published in *Educational Theory*, 2009. For full citations, please refer to the following bibliography.

Bibliography

Adorno, Theodor W. *Kant's Critique of Pure Reason*. Translated by Rodney Livingstone. Stanford: Stanford University Press, 2001.

Aoki, Ted. "Sonare and Videre: A Story, Three Echoes and a Lingering Note" (1991). In *Curriculum in a New Key: The Collected Works of Ted T. Aoki*, edited by William F. Pinar and Rita L. Irwin. Mahwah, NJ: Erlbaum, 2005.

Arendt, Hannah. *Thinking*. Vol. 1 of *The Life of the Mind*. New York: Harcourt Brace Jovanovich, 1978.

Aristotle. *Nicomachean Ethics*. Translated by Terence Irwin. Indianapolis: Hackett, 1984.

———. *Poetics*. Translated by S. H. Butcher. New York: Hill & Wang, 1961.

———. *Poetics*. Translated by James Hutton. New York: Norton, 1982.

———. *Rhetoric: The Basic Works of Aristotle*. Edited by Richard McKeon. New York: Modern Library, 2001.

Block, Alan A. *Pedagogy, Religion, and Practice: Reflections on Ethics and Teaching*. New York: Palgrave Macmillan, 2007.

———. *Talmud, Curriculum, and the Practical: Joseph Schwab and the Rabbis*. New York: Lang, 2004.

Buber, Martin. *Between Man and Man*. New York: Macmillan, 1975.

———. *I and Thou*. New York: Simon & Schuster, 1970.

Chamberlin, J. Gordon. "Phenomenological Methodology and Understanding Education." In *Existentialism and Phenomenology in Education*, edited by David E. Denton, 199–38. New York: Teachers College Press, 1974.

Chen, Xiangming. "Meaning-Making of Chinese Teachers in the Curriculum Reform." In *Autobiography and Teacher Development in China: Subjectivity in Culture in Curriculum Reform*. Edited by Zhang Hua and William F. Pinar. New York: Palgrave Macmillan, 2015.

Clarke, W. Norris. *Person and Being*. Milwaukee: Marquette University Press, 1998.

Copleston, Frederick. *A History of Philosophy*. Vol. 8. London: Burns & Oates, 1966.

Denton, David E. *Existentialism and Phenomenology in Education: Collected Essays*. New York: Teachers College Press, 1974.

Descartes, René. *Descartes' Meditations*. Edited by David B. Manley and Charles S. Taylor. http://www.wright.edu/cola/descartes/intro.html.

Duarte, Eduardo. *Being and Learning: A Poetic Phenomenology of Education*. Rotterdam: Sense, 2012.

Ellison, Ralph. *Invisible Man*. New York: Random House, 1952.

Foucault, Michel. *The Archaeology of Knowledge*. London: Routledge, 1972.

———. *Language, Counter-Memory, Practice*. Ithaca, NY: Cornell University Press, 1980.

———. *The Order of Things*. New York: Random House, 1970.

Freud, Sigmund. *Civilization and Its Discontents*. London: Hogarth, 1930.

Giorgi, Amedeo. *The Descriptive Phenomenological Method in Psychology: A Modified Husserlian Approach*. Pittsburgh: Duquesne University Press, 2009.

Gordon, Peter E. "The Place of the Sacred in the Absence of God: Charles Taylor's *A Secular Age*." *Journal of the History of Ideas* 69.4 (2008) 647–73.

Greene, Maxine. *Teacher as Stranger*. Belmont, CA: Wadsworth, 1973.

Heidegger, Martin. *Being and Time*. Translated by John Macquarrie and Edward Robinson New York: Harper and Row, 1962.

———. *The Concept of Time*. Translated by William McNeill. Cambridge, CA: Blackwell, 1992.

———. *History on the Concept of Time*. Translated by Theordore Kesiel. Bloomington: Indiana University Press, 1992.

———. *On Time and Being*. Translated by Joan Stambaugh. New York: Harper & Row, 1972.

Heschel, Abraham. *Who is Man?* Stanford, CA: Stanford University Press, 1965.

Horner, Robyn. *Rethinking God as Gift: Marion, Derrida, and the Limits of Phenomenology*. New York: Fordham University Press, 2001.

Huebner, Dwayne E. *The Lure of the Transcendent: Collected Essays by Dwayne E. Huebner*. Edited by Vikki Hillis. Mahwah, NJ: Erlbaum, 1999.

Husserl, Edmund. *The Essential Husserl*. Edited by Donn Welton. Bloomington: Indiana University Press, 1999.

Inwagen, Peter van. "The New Anti-Metaphysicians." Presidential address delivered before the one hundred sixth annual Central Division meeting of the American Philosophical Association. *Proceedings and Addresses of the American Philosophical Association* 83.2 (2009) 46–61.

James, William. *Human Immortality: Two Supposed Objections to the Doctrine*. Boston: Houghton, Mifflin, 1898.

———. *The Letters of William James*. Edited by Henry James. Boston: Boston Press, 1920.

———. *Pragmatism: A New Name for Some Old Ways of Thinking*. Boston, MA: Dover, 1956.

———. *The Principles of Psychology*. Chicago: Holt, 1952.

———. *Some Problems of Philosophy*. New York: Longmans, Green, 1940.

———. *Talks to Teachers on Psychology and to Students on Some of Life's Ideals*. New York: Holt, 1910.

———. *The Varieties of Religious Experience*. New York: Modern Library, 1936.

———. *The Will to Believe and Other Essays in Popular Philosophy*. New York: Holt, 1907.

———. *William James: Selected Unpublished Correspondence, 1885–1910*. Edited by Frederick J. Down Scott. Columbus: Ohio State University Press, 1986.

———. *Writings 1902–1910*. New York: Library of America, 1987.

Janicaud, Dominique, et al. *Phenomenology and the "Theological Turn": The French Debate*. New York: Fordham University Press, 2000.

Janouch, Gustav. *Conversations with Kafka*. New York: New Directions, 1971.

Kittler, Friedrich A. *The Truth of the Technological World: Essays on the Genealogy of Presence*. Afterword by Hans Ulrich Gumbrecht. Stanford: Stanford University Press, 2013.

Koopman, Colin. *Genealogy as Critique: Foucault and the Problems of Modernity*. Bloomington: Indiana University Press, 2013.

Kuhn, Thomas. *The Structure of Scientific Revolutions*. Chicago: University of Chicago Press, 1962.

Bibliography

Lawlor, Leonard. *Derrida and Husserl: The Basic Problem of Phenomenology*. Bloomington: Indiana University Press, 2002.

Lerner, Gerda. *Why History Matters: Life and Thought*. New York: Oxford University Press, 1997.

Luxon, Nancy. *Crisis of Authority: Politics, Trust, and Truth-Telling in Freud and Foucault*. Cambridge: Cambridge University Press, 2013.

Lyotard, Jean Francois. *Phenomenology*. Translated by Brian Beakley. New York: State University of New York, 1991.

MacIntyre, Alasdair. *After Virtue*. Notre Dame: University of Notre Dame Press, 1984.

Mann, Mary. *Life of Horace Mann*. Vol. 1. Boston: 1865.

Marion, Jean-Luc. *Being Given: Towards a Phenomenology of Givenness*. Translated by Jeffrey L. Kosky. Stanford: Stanford University Press, 2006.

———. *The Erotic Phenomenon*. Chicago: University of Chicago Press, 2007.

———. *In Excess*. Translated by Robyn Horner and Vincent Berraud. New York: Fordham University Press, 2002.

Nietzsche, Friedrich. *Basic Writings*. Edited by Walter Kaufman. New York: Modern Library, 1992.

———. *Birth of Tragedy*. Translated by Clifton P. Fadiman. Mineola, NY: Dover Thrift, 1995.

———. *Thus Spoke Zarathustra*. Translated and edited by Walter Kaufman. New York: Penguin, 1976.

Pinar, William F. *What Is Curriculum Theory?* 2nd ed. New York: Routledge, 2012.

Pinar, William F., and William Reynolds. *Understanding Curriculum as Phenomenological and Deconstructed Text*. New York: Teachers College Press, 1992.

Pinar, William F., et al. *Understanding Curriculum*. New York: Lang, 1995.

Plato. *Dialogues on Love and Friendship: Lysis, The Symposium, Phaedrus*. New York: Heritage, 1968.

Pollan, Michael. *The Botany of Desire: a Plant's Eye View of the World*. New York: Random House, 2001.

———. *In Defense of Food: An Eater's Manifesto*. New York: Penguin, 2008.

———. *The Omnivore's Dilemma: A Natural History of Four Meals*. New York: Penguin, 2006.

Ravitch, Diane. *The Death and Life of the Great American School System*. New York: Basic Books, 2011.

Richardson, Robert. *William James: In the Maelstrom of American Modernism*. New York: Mariner, 2007.

Richter, Gerhard. *Thought-Images: Frankfurt School Writers' Reflections from Damaged Life*. Stanford: Stanford University Press, 2007.

Rocha, Samuel. "Education as Mystery: The Enchanting Hope of Desire." *Educational Philosophy and Theory* 47 (in press).

———. "Educatión de Carne Hueso, Education of Flesh and Bone: Variations on Folk Melody." *Lapiz* 1 (2014) 66–77.

———. "Erotic Study: Fortune, Baby-Talk, and Jazz." *Philosophy of Education* 2012, yearbook (2012) 63–71.

———. *A Primer for Philosophy and Education*. Eugene, OR: Cascade, 2014.

———. "A Return to Love in William James and Jean-Luc Marion." *Educational Theory* 59.5 (2009) 579–88.

———. Review of *Remarks on Marx: Conversations with Duccio Trombadori*, by Michel Foucault and translated by R. James Goldstein and James Cascaito, and *Power: Essential Works of Michel Foucault 1954–1984*, by Michel Foucault and translated by Robert Hurley. *Foucault Studies* 7 (2009).

Rorty, Richard. *Philosophy and Social Hope*. New York: Penguin, 1999.

———. *Philosophy and the Mirror of Nature*. Princeton: Princeton University Press, 1979.

Ryle, Gilbert. *The Concept of Mind*. Chicago: University of Chicago Press, 1949.

Scheler, Max. *The Human Place in the Cosmos*. Evanston, IL: Northwestern University Press, 2009.

———. *Ressentiment*. Milwaukee: Marquette University Press, 2003.

Spinoza, Benedict de. *Theologico-Political Treatise*. Vol. 1 of *The Chief Works of Benedict de Spinoza*. Translated by R. H. M. Elwes. Mineola, NY: Dover, 1951.

Taylor, Charles. *The Explanation of Behavior*. London: Routledge & Kegan Paul, 1964.

———. *A Secular Age*. Cambridge: Harvard University Press, 2007.

Thoreau, Henry David. "Civil Disobedience." In *Civil Disobedience and Other Essays*. Mineola, NY: Dover Thrift, 2012.

———. "Ktaadn." In *The Maine Woods*. New York: Penguin, 1998.

Todorov, Tzvetan. *The Inner Enemies of Democracy*. Cambridge: Polity, 2014.

Wann, T. W., ed. *Behaviorism and Phenomenology: Contrasting Bases for Modern Psychology*. Chicago: University of Chicago Press, 1964.

Warnick, Bryan R. *Imitation and Education*. Albany: State University of New York Press, 2008.

Yannaras, Cristos. *Person and Eros*. Brookeline, MA: Holy Cross Orthodox Press, 2007.

Zhang, Hua, and William F. Pinar. *Autobiography and Teacher Development in China: Subjectivity and Culture in Curriculum Reform*. New York: Palgrave Macmillan, in press.

Žižek, Slavoj. *The Fragile Absolute; or, Why Is the Christian Legacy Worth Fighting For?* New York: Verso, 2000.

———. *The Puppet and the Dwarf: The Perverse Core of Christianity*. Cambridge: MIT Press, 2003.

Žižek, Slavoj, and John Milbank. *The Monstrosity of Christ*. Cambridge: MIT Press, 2009.

Index

About the Authors

Samuel D. Rocha is Assistant Professor of Philosophy of Education at the University of British Columbia. He is author of *A Primer for Philosophy and Education* (Cascade, 2014) and has released two musical works: *Freedom for Love* (indie, 2011) and *Late to Love* (Wiseblood, 2014). Rocha's next two books, forthcoming in 2016 with Cascade Books and 2017 with Springer, are both on Ivan Illich: *A Phenomenology of the Poor* and *An Apophatic Phenomenology of Education*, respectively. His companion album to this book is titled *Fear and Loving* and can be purchased on iTunes or other digital outlets.

William F. Pinar is Professor and Canada Research Chair at the University of British Columbia. Pinar has also served as the St. Bernard Parish Alumni Endowed Professor at Louisiana State University, the Frank Talbott Professor at the University of Virginia, and the A. Lindsay O'Connor Professor of American Institutions at Colgate University. He is author, most recently, of *Educational Experience as Lived* (Routledge, 2015).

Eduardo M. Duarte is Professor of Philosophy of Education and Lecturer in the Honors College at Hofstra University. He is author of *Being and Learning* (Sense, 2012) and host and producer of *The Dead Zone* and *Musings* on 88.7-WRHU, dedicated to exploring the intersections between improvisational philosophy and music.

Made in the USA
Middletown, DE
30 August 2021